HANDWRITING ANALYSIS

AN ADVENTURE IN SELF-DISCOVERY

THIRD EDITION

Peter H. Dennis

CAPCO INTERNATIONAL

HANDWRITING ANALYSIS: AN ADVENTURE IN SELF-
DISCOVERY, THIRD EDITION

ISBN 0-9698926-4-0

Cover and text design: Heidy Lawrance Associates

CAPCO INTERNATIONAL
7 Ashdown Crescent
Richmond Hill, Ontario
Canada, L4B 1Z8
Telephone: (905) 771-1543
Facsimile: (905) 771-9523
E-Mail: capco@interlog.com
Web site: www.interlog.com/~capco

Printed in Canada by Transcontinental Printing

DEDICATION

I have always admired good teachers. They are the ones who help us learn about ourselves and, in doing so, they answer a very high calling. Everyone teaches in some way and I dedicate this book to those who do it well.

ACKNOWLEDGMENTS

First, I want to express my gratitude to the six thousand or so individuals who bought the first and second editions of this book. Their purchases and positive feedback have encouraged me to build on it and to produce this third edition.

I also want to recognize my many handwriting analysis colleagues who use this book in their courses and recommend it to their students and friends. Over the years, I have had the very great pleasure of collaborating with them in study sessions, workshops, presentations and debate, and as a result, they have helped me to grow, refine my ideas, and to make this a better book. There are too many of them to name individually but mainly they are the members of the Ontario Chapter of the International Graphoanalysis Society.

PREFACE

Graphology is the term that means Handwriting Analysis. Grapho-analysis is the particular style of Graphology that is taught and practiced by the Chicago-based International Graphoanalysis Society.

Early in 1991 I became a certified Graphoanalyst and began thinking about how I might market this service. I started by telephoning a few newspaper journalists and telling them about Graphoanalysis and what it could do. Nearly all of them were at least a little intrigued and most agreed to write articles. These articles generated interest that resulted in radio and television interviews, and I soon found myself being invited to give talks on the subject.

In talking to groups, I was frequently asked if I would teach handwriting analysis. In exploring this idea, it soon became apparent that most people were not interested in becoming full-time handwriting analysts as much as they were interested in learning some of the fundamentals and gaining a few insights into themselves and others.

With this in mind, I developed a ten-hour introductory course. It has been well received, and from its inception, students began asking where they could find a book to reinforce the lessons of the course. Some encouraged me to write such a book. So I did, and here it is. The book is intended to introduce beginners to the subject, either as a companion to introductory courses or by itself. As it turned out, the book also became a popular reference for experienced practitioners.

INTRODUCTION

When starting out as a practitioner of handwriting analysis, most of us are quick to gain a great respect for its power. We learn that it gives us tremendous insight into the personality of others and , very soon, the lights go on and we realize that, more than anything, we are learning about ourselves. I think that learning about ourselves is an important part of our purpose as a species and handwriting analysis is a wonderful tool for such self-discovery.

The first edition of this book taught the reader how to do a basic analysis of personality from a sample of handwriting. It taught how to recognize over 85 different aspects of personality. The second edition presented how this knowledge could be organized so as to get a good reading in three major areas of application: emotional intelligence, compatibility in relationships and how parents and teachers could understand children better in order to help them grow and develop.

Emotional intelligence is approximately three times more important for achieving success in life, and in the workplace than is cognitive intelligence or IQ. Based on the world's first scientifically developed and validated assessment of emotional intelligence, chapter seven will show you how you can use handwriting analysis to identify fifteen key elements that make up one's EQ or Emotional Quotient. And, the good news is, that unlike IQ, EQ is learnable and growable.

When we have loving relationships in our lives, we are happier and healthier. When we have trusting, collaborative relationships in business, we can get wealthier. In other walks of life, solid, supportive relationships are important for success and well-being. I know there are exceptions but, generally, this is true.

Relationships are the most fantastic schools. Sometimes they are wonderful, they can be uplifting, developmental and joyous. Other times, they can be troublesome, dysfunctional and exasperating. In all cases, we can learn much about ourselves and then choose whether or not to make changes. Chapter eight will show you how handwriting analysis can identify some key variables to help you decide who you might want to work with, live with, marry, avoid like the plague, etc.

Over the past few years, I have heard a great many teachers and parents express frustration and alarm about the number of learning disabilities and behaviour problems they are seeing in young people. As well, many parents have told me how disappointed they are with their child's penmanship. Chapter nine deals with these and a number of related topics. Mostly, this chapter will show you how you can look at a child's handwriting and, as a parent or teacher, understand the child better and provide more appropriate support.

The third edition of this book explores a new application: Danger and Dishonesty. These are two qualities that have always intrigued humans. Who among us hasn't wondered about the honesty of someone who was trying to sell us something, persuade us of some idea or convince us to take some action? Chapter ten will show you over 60 signs that can be found in handwriting that will point to potential danger dishonesty. This is sure to give you the edge when trying to figure who is prone to lying, who is likely to cheat you and who might be a real danger.

With this new chapter and a few minor adjustments, the adventure in self-discovery continues. Enjoy.

TABLE OF CONTENTS

1

HOW TO USE THIS BOOK

—

There are at least eight ways you can use this book.

One: Read it from cover to cover.

Two: Look in the Index under a letter, e.g. the letter i. The Index tells you that i appears on six different pages, 50, 65, 72, 87, 174 and 187. On each of these pages you can compare the i shown with yours, and if they are similar, you can learn the meaning and apply it to yourself. If your i's are like the ones on page 50, you are likely good at detail. If they are like the ones on page 65, chances are you like to stand out from the crowd. If they are like those on page 72, you may be irritable. And, if they are like the ones on page 87, could you be a procrastinator? You get the idea.

Three: You can also look in the Index and find a personality trait that you are interested in. Look it up and see if the handwriting strokes on the page match yours.

Four: You might go to the worksheet in Chapter Six and take each trait in turn. Look them up and see if and how much they apply to you. Do this for each trait and you will have a very comprehensive analysis of your personality.

Five: If you want to learn more about your emotional intelligence, go directly to Chapter Seven.

Six: If you want to learn more about relationships and compatibility, see Chapter Eight.

Seven: If you are a parent or teacher, or otherwise have an interest in children, Chapter Nine will give you some helpful things to think about that you likely didn't encounter in teachers' college or in parenting courses.

Eight: If you work in a business, develop relationships or other-wise engage in life, it can be a great comfort to know who is being honest and who can be trusted. Chapter Ten will show you how to look at handwriting and identify who has the potential to be dangerous and who is being less than honest.

2

SOME FREQUENTLY
ASKED QUESTIONS

—

WHAT ARE THE ORIGINS OF HANDWRITING ANALYSIS?

No one knows for sure where or when it started. Some speculate that it started soon after handwriting was invented. The earliest written references are found in the works of Aristotle where some of his musings about handwriting are interpreted by certain observers as commentary on handwriting analysis. I'm not so sure; they seem a little ambiguous to me.

It is generally accepted, however, that the first serious treatise on handwriting analysis was written in 1622 by Camillo Baldi, a professor at the University of Bologna. The next noteworthy treatment followed in the late 18th century by the Swiss scholar of personality, Johann Kasper Lavater. During the 19th century, many members of the French clergy studied the subject and most notable among them was Abbe Jean–Hippolyte Michon who gave us the term, "graphologie." By the end of that century, a number of German scientists had become involved and they provided many new findings and insights.

Just after the beginning of the 20th century, Alfred Binet, the inventor of the I.Q. test, conducted some of the first validation studies at the Sorbonne in Paris. Under his scrutiny, analysts were able to correctly identify successful men considerably better than chance. As well, he had some success in discerning intelligence and honesty.

Since then, many scientists, artists, philosophers, intellectuals and other notables have investigated handwriting analysis and have commented favourably about it. Among them are: Jung, Freud, Gainsborough, Goethe, Poe, the Brownings, Balzac, Dickens and Einstein, to name a few.

Today, there are many individuals and organizations engaged in research and teaching. As well, there is now a proliferation of graphological web sites, chat groups and bookstores on the Internet.

IS HANDWRITING ANALYSIS SCIENTIFIC?

To fully satisfy the criteria of scientific validity, a study must be published so that one's professional peers may have the opportunity of examining, challenging and replicating the study. In this strict sense, handwriting analysis generally falls short. There are some studies that meet these criteria but these are relatively few.

This does not mean that handwriting analysis isn't valid. It just means that, overall, the validity of the subject has not yet been proven to the satisfaction of the scientific community.

This is not an easy thing to do as it takes a great deal of time and money to conduct and publish appropriate studies. As well, like many subjects dealing with human beings, e.g. psychology, sociology or medicine, some aspects might be highly scientific and valid while others are clearly not. And, to confuse the issue further, handwriting analysis is highly dependent upon the skill of the individual practitioner.

In spite of these difficulties, validation studies continue to go on. Many of the individuals and organizations conducting these studies do so primarily to satisfy their own purposes. They do not publish their results for peer review and thus fall short of fully satisfying the scientific model.

An example is the International Graphoanalysis Society which has had a research department in place from 1929. Through its recent history that department was headed by Dr. James C. Crumbaugh, who was the "Mississippi Psychologist of the Year" in 1989. Dr. Crumbaugh, in a reprint entitled: *Graphoanalytic Cues,* originally published in *The Encyclopedia of Clinical Assessment, volume II, 1980, pp. 919–929,* points to a number of studies that: "seem to be the most effective in demonstrating a scientific basis for the assumption that handwriting can be as valid in personality assessment as the other major projective techniques." An example of a projective technique would be the Rorschach Inkblot Test.

Although it seems a little circumspect to me, this statement suggests a degree of optimism and I believe Dr. Crumbaugh was saying that these studies demonstrate a reasonable basis for assuming that the possibility of scientific validation exists.

So, it seems that although many studies have been done by reputable individuals and organizations, there have not been enough of them done to the degree necessary for general acceptance as scientifically valid.

Again, this doesn't mean that handwriting analysis isn't valid. It just means that it hasn't been scientifically proven to be fully valid, at this point in time. Of course, on the other hand, many of us who are practicing handwriting analysis have our own studies and reasons for believing that a substantial amount of it is very highly valid. As well, a considerable number of psychologists, psychiatrists, physicians and other professionals have enough confidence in handwriting analysis to have learned about it and to actively use it.

WHAT ARE SOME OF THE USES OF HANDWRITING ANALYSIS?

Perhaps the most interesting and valuable use of handwriting analysis is that of learning more about ourselves. Many people think that this may be our primary purpose in life. If it isn't, it is still one that seems to capture the interest of nearly everyone and, if you doubt this, just look at the magazine counters and bookshelves. Even when we are helping others to learn something about themselves, are they not reflecting things that give us further insights into ourselves?

Handwriting analysis can play an important role whenever it is useful to know something about human personality. Here are a few examples of how it can be used:

- Personnel Selection—Inputs for making decisions about new hires, promotions, transfers and terminations.
- Compatibility Analysis—Can be used for putting together a small team of compatible individuals to work together on a group project. It could be helpful for two or three prospective business partners as well as for two people contemplating marriage.
- Career Guidance—Knowing strengths, weaknesses, aptitudes and hidden talents relative to the requirements of specific careers can be invaluable.
- Saving psychologists, psychiatrists and psychotherapists a great deal of "couch time."
- Enabling teachers to identify the strengths, weaknesses, aptitudes and talents that contribute to or detract from their students' learning.
- Supporting social workers and counselors in identifying and dealing with their clients' behaviours and personalities.
- Helping buyers, sellers and other negotiators to identify ways that they might present points, argue positions and deal with conflict.
- Assisting law enforcement agencies in the detection of crimes and in identifying suspects.
- Prompting credit officers to ask more probing questions and enhance their investigations when analysis reveals an individual who may be a poor credit risk.

HOW SHOULD HANDWRITING ANALYSIS BE USED IN EMPLOYEE SELECTION?

My recommendation to employers who are serious about selecting people is to build a solid package of valid and reliable selection instruments designed to accommodate the specific needs of the organization and the requirements of the job.

Such a package might include testing for skills, interests, mental abilities and temperament; planned and effective interviews; thorough reference checks; and handwriting analysis.

Most important, do not make decisions based on any one instrument. Base them instead on the information gathered from the total package. If one instrument's results stand out from the trend, dig deeper and ask more questions. Then, when all the inputs are gathered and the questions are resolved, make your decision.

How does handwriting analysis compare to other selection tools? Interestingly, the research on employment interviews shows that they generally have poor validity ratings (not much better than chance). However, when interviewers are properly trained and prepare well for the interview, the validity rises dramatically.

As far as selection tests go, Canada does not have legislation requiring tests to be valid. Consequently, there is a lot of what I consider to be "junk" on the market, to the detriment of both employers and candidates.

So, how does handwriting analysis compare? Usually, quite favorably. Its information is especially useful prior to an interview or reference check because it can alert you to some very pertinent questions.

What is a good way to communicate to candidates the fact that you are going to have their handwriting analyzed? Simply tell them. Tell them that you will interview them, you will be conducting certain tests, you will be checking references and you will be getting an analysis of their handwriting. Tell them that you will take all of these inputs into account and make the best decision you can so as to achieve the best possible job match.

HOW DOES THE LAW VIEW HANDWRITING ANALYSIS?

Federal and provincial Human Rights and Employment Standards legislation are all silent on the use of handwriting analysis as a selection tool. So, in Canada and in its provinces, there is nothing in the acts or codes to say that handwriting analysis cannot be used.

I have not examined the jurisprudence of other countries in this regard, and therefore have to restrict my comments to Canada. I know, however, that handwriting analysis is used in many western countries as a selection tool and I suspect that most employers are responsible and choose to operate within the law.

If the validity of the practice is ever seriously challenged in the courts, I am sure that a great debate would follow about the various types and degrees of validity and how they are determined. I'll pass on predicting any outcomes.

Another point: Handwriting analysis is very clean with respect to the usual grounds for discrimination because it seems unable to reveal race, gender, religion, age, creed, family status or many of the other prohibited areas.

I suppose some day someone might allege employment discrimination on the grounds that he or she was denied a job because of handwriting analysis. This would be a tough one to win as there is no current Canadian legislation requiring selection tools to be valid. The individual would probably have to make a case that one of the prohibited grounds, e.g. race, religion, etc., was the basis for the discrimination, and so far, handwriting analysis doesn't seem capable of identifying many of these.

As we know, anything is possible and laws do change but an employer could avoid much hassle by ensuring that handwriting analysis is used as one component in a package of selection tools as I recommended above.

CAN AN ANALYSIS OF HANDWRITING PREDICT THE FUTURE?

This question is not as preposterous as you might think. I have had it directed to me many times and it is not uncommon to see handwriting analysts set up shop at psychic fairs. As well, some analysts freely admit to using their intuition to glean impressions from the script.

So, against that background, here's my answer: An analysis of handwriting will not directly predict the future. I happen to believe in human free will and hold that, for the most part, we have the ability to choose the actions that we take. I suspect that those who do predict the future, are somehow tapping into how our choices are trending and are reading the probabilities about what may happen as a result. In effect, our future is not determined until we determine it; it depends on how we manage our choices.

Whether you believe that or not, you would probably agree that the more we know about an individual, the more we are able to make reasonable predictions about how he or she might behave under a certain set of circumstances.

For example, who is more likely to be the better manager, A or B? A sets high goals, she has strong will power, determination, persistence and tenacity. She is outgoing, likes people, thinks efficiently and has good control of her emotions. She is enthusiastic, intuitive, assertive and takes initiative. B, on the other hand, is weak in all of these areas and, in addition, is evasive, deceptive, argumentative, disorganized and emotionally unstable.

In this example, we really cannot predict with certainty who is going to be the better future manager but, based on the foregoing short analysis, and, with all else being equal, the probabilities are that A will be a better manager than B. To some degree then, handwriting analysis can give us insights that will help us to predict a probable future.

WHAT CONSTITUTES A PROPER HANDWRITING SAMPLE?

Here are the guidelines for an ideal sample:

- Use unlined paper and have a few sheets under the one you are writing on. This way the analyst can get a fair idea of how much pressure you are putting on the paper.
- If at all possible, provide an original document as opposed to photocopies or facsimiles.
- Use a ball-point or fountain pen. Pencils, felt-tip and roller ball pens are not as effective when determining pressure, strengh of will and certain other traits.
- If you have the choice, use black ink instead of any other color; it copies best and produces the best facsimiles.
- What you write should be spontaneous. It should not be copied or memorized.
- Sample size should be at least one 8½" by 11" page. A larger sample is usually better.
- It is ideal if the analyst can see or at least understand the circumstances under which the sample was written. For example, were conditions peaceful or distracting, were there interruptions, was the writer in a hurry, were there any difficulties with the pen or ink? etc.
- I usually ask the writer to write some words that give me permission to do an analysis of his or her writing and then sign and date the sample.

What if the sample falls short of this ideal? In simple terms then, the chances are that the analysis will also fall short of the ideal. What you are doing here is looking at certain strokes in the writing and making judgments about the personality traits that they may indicate. If the strokes are not enough to be representative of the individual, then you risk a faulty analysis.

For example, defiance is indicated by abnormally high k–buckles. If there are no k's in your sample, then you cannot get a reading for defiance. Similarly, as balanced f's indicate organizational ability and you have only one f in the sample, you do not have a statistically representative sample. For all you know, someone might have bumped the desk just as the writer was forming that lonely f. That's why at least one full page is important and, for some purposes, more would be required.

HOW GOOD ARE ANALYSES OF SIGNATURES?

The previous section lets you know that a decent sample should be at least a page in length. A signature, being one, two or three words, falls considerably short.

On the other hand, we probably practice and perfect our signature more than any other element of our writing. If our handwriting represents us at all, wouldn't our signature represent us best?

As you can see, there is a little conflict in these two positions. On the one hand, a signature is a small sample and it does lack the full range of stroke structures that are necessary for a full analysis. On the other hand, for its size, it is a sample that can tell us a great deal about the writer.

Our signature is our trademark and it reflects the personality that we portray to the public. Our regular script represents our real or private self. Sometimes the two are different, almost as if written by two different people. This shouldn't be too surprising because we all know people who act differently in public than they do in private.

I believe that an analyst can glean quite a bit from a signature but I caution that, not only will many stroke structures be missing but the signature may not be representative of the writer in other ways. At the moment the signature was written, for example, someone could have bumped into the desk, the pen could have run out of ink, the writer might have been distracted, etc.

There are people, however, who specialize in signature analysis and, with relatively little to go on, they can develop a pretty elaborate analysis. They will look at the placement of the signature relative to the end of the writing and relative to the left or right margin. They will compare the size of the signature with the size of the script. They will interpret the degree of legibility and the use of initials versus full names. They will look at underlining, overscoring, crossing out and conflicting slants.

In spite of this, analyzing a signature is still pretty limited and should never be portrayed as a full analysis. It can reveal some personality traits but remember, the stroke structures are too few and they may not be representative of the writer.

This discussion brings up a related and very practical point. If a signature isn't necessarily representative of the writer and if the stroke structures are too few to paint a complete picture, then isn't there some risk in displaying signatures or short handwritten phrases in advertising or in other aspects of business?

Elaine Charal (a friend and colleague) and I were once given a few products by *Marketing Magazine* and asked to do an analysis of the signatures and script used on the labels. We had John Labatt, President's Choice, Orville Redenbacher and a few others. We did our analysis which *Marketing* published on March 22, 1993. In a number of instances, we were kind.

On another occasion I spent an afternoon in a library looking at the auditor signatures in annual reports. I found many admirable traits in these signatures but I also found deceit, evasiveness, procrastination, inattention to detail and other traits that the accounting firms probably did not want to project. *The Financial Post* had fun with this on February 6, 1992.

My point in mentioning these two experiences is to suggest that there is some degree of risk in using handwriting, and especially signatures, to promote products and services. In North America, this is becoming more of an issue and business people would be well advised to consult a handwriting analyst before supporting their marketing efforts with a favorite script. This is advisable for three reasons.

First, handwriting contains many universal symbols that send messages on an unconscious level, e.g. sharp, angled writing suggests impatience, anger or aggressiveness; rounded writing conveys softness or friendliness; big writing suggests extrovert and small, introvert, etc. Second, more books, courses, articles and information are being disseminated on the subject. And third, in our global economy, we are dealing more with countries where the citizens are considerably more knowledgeable about handwriting analysis.

WHAT ELSE IS IMPORTANT TO KNOW?

You might have noticed that this isn't a frequently asked question. I put it in, however, because I wanted to draw your attention clearly to two important points before we go charging off to do our analysis.

My first point is that "no trait stands alone." This means that the interpretation of any single stroke of handwriting must take into account all other related strokes from the same sample. Humans are very complex and analyzing their personalities cannot not be done accurately by simply identifying a list of individual traits in isolation from each other.

Here's what I mean. Suppose we have two writers who have each provided a sample of handwriting where, in each case, about one third of their a's and o's are about equally open. Page 104 tells us that these strokes indicate "Talkativeness."

Upon looking further, we find that one writer's script shows strong indications of introversion, conservatism, caution, timidity, self-consciousness and low self-esteem. The other writer's script shows none of these traits and we see exceptionally high degrees of extroversion, emotional responsiveness, self-confidence, humour and egomania.

On the basis of the open a's and o's alone, we would probably have declared that these two writers are about equally talkative. But after taking the additional traits into account, it no longer makes sense to maintain this same interpretation.

So, before you pronounce that "this means that," look around the sample and see what else you can find to either support or reduce that conclusion.

My second point is, whenever possible, observe the writer as he/she is writing the sample you are about to analyze. Failing this, ask about the conditions under which the sample was written.

Generally speaking, we are able to do a superior analysis when we know the conditions under which a sample was written. For example, what if a writer was using a faulty pen, or had just emerged from a traffic accident or was minding three energetic young people while producing the sample on the living room floor?

So with these two points in mind, be careful and remember that this book is only an introduction to a very complex subject. It will give you some interesting insights into yourself and others. It will give you lots to think about, and at times you will be able to dazzle your friends. On that basis, have fun with the book, enjoy the adventure of self–discovery but treat it all with a little humility and leave the heavy-duty analysis to the pros.

3

THE EMOTIONS

If this book is about self—discovery then fundamental to that adventure is learning about our emotions. They colour so much of what we do and how we do it, they mire us in depression and despair and they drive us to achievement and glory.

If you doubt this, the next time you watch the Olympics, the Commonwealth Games, the Stanley Cup playoffs, etc. just listen to the athletes describe what they believe success is all about and what drives them. For the most part, they are describing emotions and, in their sport, they are discovering a great deal about themselves. So, whether it is athletics or any other worthwhile pursuit, it is largely the emotions that we are dealing with and, in so doing, we are getting much closer to who we are.

To that end, handwriting analysis can tell us a good deal about the emotions and how they influence nearly all of the personality traits that this book deals with.

To pursue this subject, it is important to make a distinction between two terms: **emotional responsiveness** and **emotional expressiveness**. The former is an individual's capacity to respond to that which arouses the emotions. An emotionally responsive person, for example, is one who would feel moved by a sad story more than the average person.

This is different from emotional expressiveness which is the degree to which an individual outwardly shows or expresses his or her internal response to an emotional situation. For example, the emotionally expressive person might weep when hearing the sad story.

An individual, therefore, could be emotionally responsive without necessarily being emotionally expressive, because he or she has developed controls and has learned to suppress or inhibit expression. This could happen, for example, in a corporate setting where the expression of emotions might be frowned upon.

The degree to which an individual is emotionally responsive is determined by measuring the **slant** of the writing. Slant can be deceptive to the casual eye, so first I will show you the correct procedure for measuring it and then I will explain what different degrees of slant mean.

Here's the procedure:

- Correctly, you should draw and measure about 100 consecutive angles of slant, ideally taken from somewhere near the middle of the writing sample. You should use a sharp, thin-leaded pencil and a straight-edged ruler.
- To determine an angle of slant, you must first draw a base line for each letter involved in the 100 angles. A base line is an imaginary horizontal line upon which a letter sits. It is constructed by joining the starting point of the approach stroke to the ending point of the last downstroke (see A and B below). Where there is no approach stroke, the ending point of the last downstroke of the previous letter may be taken along with the next base line point (C). Where there is no preceding letter, such a point may be estimated, taking into account the general line of the writing (D).

| A | B | C | D |

- After the base lines are drawn, the slant lines are next. They are straight lines, drawn only for upstrokes that begin at or intersect a base line and rise to at least the average height of the lower case letters. They begin where the pen leaves the base line and they end at the highest point of the upstroke.

for example:

baseline

- To make measurement easier, extend the slant lines above the tops of the letters as well as below the base lines. Like so:

baseline

- Now comes the task of measuring the angle between the base line and the slant line. This requires an instrument known as a Slant Gauge (The International Graphoanalysis Society) or an Emotional Dial (The Oseka Machine Company). Other Manufacturers may have different names for something similar. The idea is that such an instrument can line up the base line and the slant line and produce a reading that indicates the angle of slant and, thus, the degree of emotional responsiveness of the stroke being measured. Here's an example of what one might look like:

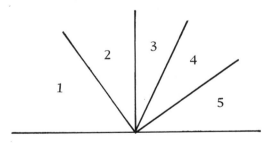

Base Line

- You can see from this, if you line up the base line and the slant line, each slant line will fall into one of the five areas. When you do this for 100 slant lines, you get a trend or a pattern. You might find, for example, that one writer has 75% of her strokes in area 4, 20% in area 3 and 5% in area 5. You will get many different patterns but most writers will have slant lines that fall predominately into one or two areas. The more areas that are covered, the more the writer exhibits varying responsiveness.

Each area is indicative of a different degree of emotional responsiveness and can be characterized as follows:

1. These writers lack emotional responsiveness, are likely to display little feeling and can be very self-centered.
2. These writers also lack emotional responsiveness, don't display feelings and exhibit some amount of self- interest.
3. These writers are mildly responsive to their emotions, they are objective and are primarily driven by logic and judgment. You can say that their heads will usually rule their hearts.
4. These writers are generally responsive to their emotions while maintaining good judgment. They show their feelings easily and still preserve objectivity.
5. These writers are highly responsive to their emotions and the heart nearly always rules the head.

In summary, slant is a measure of emotional responsiveness. The farther the slant leans to the right, the more the writer is emotionally responsive, ruled by the heart and likely an extrovert. The more upright or vertical the slant, the more the writer is ruled by the head, is objective and relies on judgment and logic. The more we see a back slant or a leaning to the left, the more the individual displays a lack of feelings and tends to be self–interested.

Depth is the term used to describe the heaviness or pressure put onto the page. The heavier the writing, the deeper and longer lasting are the emotions. Someone with heavy writing will remember emotional events and feelings longer and feel them more strongly than the average person. These people love, hate and carry prejudices with more intensity.

So, someone with a forward or right-leaning slant as well as heavy writing is emotionally responsive and has lasting feelings.

In addition to indicating lasting feelings, depth identifies two other qualities: Sensuousness and energy level. By sensuousness I mean that the heavy writer has more acute senses and can feel, smell, see, taste and hear more sensitively than most others. They see colors more vividly, hear sounds more fully, etc.

Energy level is greater when the writing is heavier. So, a proverbial axe murderer with heavy strokes is more dangerous than one who brushes the page lightly. Here are examples of depth:

light moderate

heavy

very heavy

In summary, depth is the weight or pressure put on the page. It is an indicator of three things: emotional memory, sensuousness and energy level. The heavier the writing the more each of these are present in the writer.

Because depth is the measure of pressure on the page, feeling the impression that the pen has made upon the paper can be helpful. This is one reason why photocopies and facsimiles are not as desirable as original samples.

4

THINKING

In handwriting analysis, an understanding of the emotions is of primary importance. The second key area to understand is how the individual thinks. Here our focus is not on what people think but on how they think: what methods they use, how alert and quick they are and how they go about solving problems. We want to know about their style of thinking.

Realistically, no two people think in exactly the same way but there are some overall styles of thinking that handwriting analysis can identify. For our purposes there are four broad categories or styles of thinking: cumulative, investigative, exploratory and comprehensive. Few of us rely exclusively on any one style, yet for most of us, one style is dominant. Let's look at each of them.

Cumulative Thinking:

These thinkers are builders. They like to build one fact or idea upon another until enough are gathered to reach a conclusion. Although these folks appear to be slower than other thinkers, this is no reflection on intelligence (Thomas Edition's writing indicated this style of thinking). They are careful, they don't jump to conclusions and, in the thinking world, they might be characterized as the tortoises because they often win the race by being right.

Cumulative thinking is identified in the writing by m's and n's that are wide and have rounded tops, much like the ones that were taught in elementary school. Usually these structures are accompanied by broad R's and wide circle letters. Here are some examples:

come home now

Cumulative

Investigative Thinking:

These people want to know all about everything that has been discovered. They want to know how things work, what makes them tick and why.

Investigative thinking is found in the writing where the tops of m's and n's are more pointed than rounded and where the m's and n's are not as wide as in cumulative thinking. Slender, sharp tops indicate the writer's willingness to probe deeply into a subject, whereas, m's and n's that are wider at the base line and more rounded at the top indicate less interest in deep inquiry.

Here are some examples of investigative writing. Example A shows the writing of someone interested in learning about a subject in depth. Example B shows interest in learning enough to be conversant or to satisfy short–term needs and C shows casual curiosity.

A   B   C

You will notice that examples A, B and C all have sharp points on the tops. Investigative thinking, although very often this way, can also have tops that are slightly rounded. When rounded tops appear on investigative writing, the mounds on the m's and n's must be much narrower than the wider cumulative strokes, like so:

Rounded Investigative

Exploratory Thinking:

As the investigative thinkers want to know about things that are known or discovered, exploratory thinkers want to know about the unknown. For example, an investigator might want to know all about dentistry and an explorer might want to discover the origin of the universe. As well, explorers usually want to find out things for themselves. Tell them the paint is wet and they will want to touch it.

Exploratory thinking is indicated in the handwriting much like investigative thinking. The difference is that the tops of the m's and n's rise above the tops of the other lower–case letters. Here is an illustration to show the difference:

Investigative   **Exploratory**

Comprehensive Thinking:

This is sometimes referred to as keen or quick comprehension. These are fast thinkers, they catch on quickly and they are bright. If the cumulative thinkers are the tortoises of the thinking world, then these are the hares. When you are in mid–explanation of something, they are saying or thinking: "Yeah, yeah, I've got it." The ironic thing is that sometimes they haven't "got it." They can be hasty in reaching conclusions and, although they may be very bright, they can some-times be careless and jump to a wrong one.

Comprehensive thinking is seen in retraced upstrokes on m's and n's. These structures often look like u's or w's and are needle–like in appearance. Here are some examples:

Comprehensive

As stated above, most people have one predominant thinking style. However it is not uncommon to see more than one style in a writer's script. The good news is that the more thinking styles one has, the more different ways one can approach mental challenges. People with more than one style are often better problem-solvers.

There is more that handwriting analysis can tell us about thinking than just thinking styles. How we process information, make evaluations and sort out the important from the unimportant is called **analytical ability**. Analytical ability causes us to pause and evaluate as we think and thus arrive at conclusions that are more sound and accurate.

Wedges that point downward to the base line in m's and n's are indicative of analytical ability. As the wedge becomes sharper, the analysis becomes more penetrating. To fully qualify, the wedges must have no retracing and they must meet the base line. In the three examples that follow, only A demonstrates analytical ability; B does not touch the base line and C is retraced.

| A | B | C |

Another aspect of thinking is fluidity. This is a quality that you can recognize when you are in its presence. You see it in dance, athletics, speech and many other areas of activity. It happens when things are going smoothly and gracefully and when changes can be made quickly and easily, without missing a beat. Wayne Gretzky is a fluid skater, Karen Kain is a fluid dancer, Pierre Trudeau can be a fluid orator. When they are "on," they make it look easy. They glide, it's beautiful. You know what I mean.

Well, it's the same with thinking. The ideas come steadily and they flow easily, one into the other, there's no hesitation. Some people have this gift and the rest of us may experience it on occasion.

In handwriting, **fluidity of thought** is seen in figure–eight strokes, typically, in g's, f's s's, and you can find it where one letter flows smoothly into the next. An example would be a t–bar that becomes the lead–in to an h in the word the. Here are some fluidity strokes:

Fluidity of Thought

When you put a few **basic traits** together and develop a conclusion from the composite, you have an **evaluated trait**. This book is not going to deal with evaluated traits but for one exception. It's called **intellectual efficiency**. It is an indication of how well an individual uses his or her mental capacity. It is not intelligence but it is somewhat dependent on intelligence.

The elements making up this evaluated trait are: comprehensive thinking, intuitiveness, creativity, attention to detail, decisiveness, fluidity of thought, as well as challenging goals and a strong sense of purpose (willpower). All of these basic traits are easily discernible in handwriting and most are explained in chapter five.

You can imagine that if an individual possesses all of these basic traits, it would follow that he/she is an efficient thinker. I wanted to use this example not only to point out that there is more to thinking than what's been covered so far, but to show how an evaluated trait works and how it is possible to combine a number of basic traits and come to a larger conclusion.

A final note on thinking. People think differently in different circumstances. We saw before that, generally speaking, higher, sharper wedges mean deeper and more penetrating thinking. Wouldn't it then follow that, generally speaking, lower or more shallow wedges point to rather superficial thinking?

Not necessarily. When many people are in a hurry, their writing tends to flatten out. Also, when you have a lot of boring or repetitive writing to do, you tend to get sloppy and shallow. My point here is that an artful analyst would consider these possibilities and perhaps conclude that, temporarily, this writer was either hurried, bored, not paying much attention or in a somewhat superficial mood.

As analysts, it is important that we get a sample of the writer's typical script so that our analysis will be truly representative of the writer.

5

75 PERSONALITY TRAITS

This section introduces the reader to seventy–five different personality traits. Each trait is defined and then described in three ways that it can show itself positively and three ways in which it might manifest negatively. This is followed by an explanation and an illustration of how the trait can be identified.

ACQUISITIVENESS

Concept:
A desire or urge to acquire, obtain or possess. The objects of acquisitiveness may be tangible or intangible, and they can include knowledge or ideas as well as material possessions.

Positively Directed:
- Collecting stamps, coins, antiques, etc.
- Taking courses to acquire more knowledge.
- Owning an extensive library.

Negatively Directed:
- Fraud, embezzlement, shoplifting, etc.
- Desiring things that are beyond one's reach.
- Greed, avarice, selfishness.

Indication:
Hooks found at the beginning of a stroke. Usually they are found at the beginning of a word. Sometimes they are found within a word. As the object of the acquisitiveness becomes more important to the writer the hooks become larger.

Illustrations:

I will take it

AGGRESSIVENESS

Concept:
A driving force or energy directed towards the achievement of a goal. It can involve unprovoked attack and domination of others.

Positively Directed:
- Employing strong initiative to accomplish a task.
- Using proactive, legal tactics in a sporting event.
- Strongly taking the initiative in an advertising campaign.

Negatively Directed:
- Launching an unprovoked attack on another country.
- Cut-throat competition in business.
- Physically or verbally attacking another individual.

Indication:
A strong move of the upstroke that breaks sharply away from the downstroke and drives up and to the right. Found below the base line, in f, g, j, p, q and y.

Illustrations:

aggressive player

ARGUMENTATIVENESS

Concept:

Excessive arguing or raising of objections. Arguing for the sake of arguing.

Positively Directed:

- Helps others to recognize their errors.
- Literary criticism.
- Enthusiastic participation in discussions and debates.

Negatively Directed:

- Reduces attention to what others are saying.
- Compels one to always have the last word.
- Takes exception to almost everything.

Indication:

The beginning of the downstroke on a small letter p starts at a point higher than the buckle that is formed after the completion of the upstroke. This can occur whether or not there is an approach stroke.

Illustrations:

appropriate   perform

ATTENTION, DESIRE FOR

Concept:
The urge to attract the notice, recognition, approval, affection or appreciation of others.

Positively Directed:
- Doesn't shy away from the spotlight.
- Promotes oneself easily.
- May direct some energy toward helping others.

Negatively Directed:
- Can upstage others in order to be recognized.
- Behavior can be disruptive to a team.
- Can be extravagant in order to attract attention.

Indication:
The final stroke of a word that rises higher than the height of the lower–case letters and curves upward and backward.

Illustrations:

BROAD–MINDEDNESS

Concept:
Tolerant of the opinions, ideas, thoughts, views or behaviors of others. Free from bigotry and prejudice.

Positively Directed:
- Pays attention to what others are saying.
- Takes a variety of opinions into account.
- Sees both sides of an argument.

Negatively Directed:
- May interfere with decision making.
- Could lead to gullibility.
- Could contribute to confusion.

Indication:
Found in broad e's. Can be reinforced by round circle letters, e.g., a, o.

Illustrations:

seems open to me

CAUTION

Concept:
A carefulness, wariness or concern for avoiding injury or misfortune. A hesitation to take risks.

Positively Directed:
- Minimizes risk.
- Takes all circumstances into account before deciding.
- Avoids hasty decisions or actions.

Negatively Directed:
- May never take a risk.
- Slow to initiate action.
- May start too late.

Indication:
Displayed by long, straight final strokes at the end of a line.

Illustrations:

please be careful

don't go near

CHANGE, DESIRE FOR

Concept:
An urge for change in surroundings, tasks, or activities.

Positively Directed:
- Can adapt easily to a changing environment.
- Likely to gain broad and varied experience.
- Not likely to get stuck in a rut.

Negatively Directed:
- Generally not good at performing routine tasks.
- Not likely to stay long in a routine job.
- Although experience may be varied, it may not be deep.

Indication:
Found in long downstrokes occurring below the base line. The longer the downstroke, the greater the writer's desire for change. For this trait to be indicated, the length of the downstroke must be at least three times the height of the lower–case letters. It doesn't matter if there is a loop attached to the downstroke or not.

Illustrations:

always changing

CLANNISHNESS

Concept:
Banding together in small, exclusive groups. The choice of friends is usually limited to one or two.

Positively Directed:
- Friends are carefully chosen.
- Friendships are deep and highly valued.
- High level of trust and commitment to the chosen few.

Negatively Directed:
- Can miss out on the ideas, contacts, experiences, etc. that a larger number of friends can provide.
- Can be possessive of friends.
- Risks alienating those who are excluded.

Indication:
Small loops at the bottom of downstrokes.

Illustrations:

hardly any amigos

CONCENTRATION

Concept:

The habit of avoiding distractions and intensely focusing one's complete attention on a single task, problem or activity.

Positively Directed:

- Operates well as a specialist.
- Performs well at small, precise tasks, e.g. electronic assembly, jeweler, watchmaker.
- Doesn't usually miss details.

Negatively Directed:

- Can miss seeing the bigger picture.
- Can be oblivious to what is happening around the activity at hand.
- Not likely to be a generalist.

Indication:

Writing is consistently small and lower–case writing must be no higher than ⅟₁₆th of an inch.

Illustrations:

tiny and focused writing

CONFUSION OF INTERESTS

Concept:
Involvement in too many activities at one time so as to compromise effectiveness.

Positively Directed:
- Has a great variety of interests, ideas and activities.
- Is seldom idle or looking for things to do.
- Usually willing to take on another task or project.

Negatively Directed:
- Often takes on more than he/she can handle effectively.
- Can have difficulty meeting deadlines.
- Can jump from task to task, leaving some unfinished.

Indication:
Confusion of interest occurs when the lower loops of one line intertwine with the upper loops of the next line.

Illustrations:

DECEIT

Concept:
The act of concealing or misrepresenting the truth. This can be achieved through words or actions. It may be done intentionally or unintentionally.

Positively Directed:
- Can put a positive light on a negative situation.
- In a sales situation, emphasizes the positive points.
- Maintains good relations by telling people what they want to hear.

Negatively Directed:
- Misrepresents the truth (intentionally or unintentionally).
- Distorts or omits details.
- May not disclose the negative side of a situation.

Indication:
Approach strokes and final strokes both form loops within circle letters (a's, o's and g's).

Illustrations:

can't go to bank

DECISIVENESS

Concept:
The ability to arrive at a judgment, conclusion or decision.

Positively Directed:
- Moves easily from thinking to acting.
- Knows clearly what he/she wants and moves towards it.
- Takes a firm stand once a decision is reached.

Negatively Directed:
- Can be hasty in decision making.
- In the absence of good thinking, decisions can be driven largely by the emotions.
- May make decisions without gathering the necessary input or consensus of others.

Indication:
Found on final strokes with firm endings.

Illustrations:

make up your mind

DEFIANCE

Concept:
A disposition to challenge, disregard, show contempt, oppose or resist authority or opposition.

Positively Directed:
- Will oppose what he/she perceives as injustice.
- In a confrontation, will fight rather than run.
- Will challenge ideas before accepting them.

Negatively Directed:
- Has difficulty abiding by the rules.
- Could be uncooperative.
- Finds it difficult to ask for help.

Indication:
Found where the buckle on a lower-case k is higher than other lower-case letters. Other inflated buckles can also indicate this trait, e.g. capital R's, capital B's and small p's. This trait can also be found in printing.

Illustrations:

look at the book

DETAIL, ATTENTION TO

Concept:
An awareness of and focus on each aspect, item or point. A recognition that each of the small elements is important to the whole.

Positively Directed:
- Reduces errors.
- Improves quality and accuracy.
- Enhances the memory of past events and experiences.

Negatively Directed:
- Can lose sight of the larger, overall picture.
- Can become an obsession and interfere with job completion or meeting deadlines.
- Can contribute to "nit-picking."

Indication:
Indicated when the dots of i's and j's are placed close to the stems. Carefully formed and consistent writing reinforces this trait.

Illustrations:

his liking for animals

DETERMINATION

Concept:
Steady, continuous action towards a goal or purpose. Resolve or staying power.

Positively Directed:
- Contributes to job completion.
- Enhances endurance.
- Doesn't abandon the goal or give up easily.

Negatively Directed:
- Can be obsessive or fanatical about completing what has been started.
- May not notice changing circumstances while pushing ahead.
- May not know when to let go or quit.

Indication:
Indicated when down–strokes below the base line are thicker than the rest of the writing. The thickness indicates the degree of force of determination while the length indicates the endurance or staying power of the determination.

Illustrations:

going my way

DIGNITY

Concept:

The state of feeling worthy or honorable because one's thoughts and conduct are based on particular standards and principles.

Positively Directed:
- Controls the expression of emotions.
- Contributes to integrity.
- Lends objectivity and poise to emotional situations.

Negatively Directed:
- May not express feelings easily.
- Detracts from spontaneity.
- Lacks sensitivity to legitimate criticism.

Indication:

Retraced t and d stems.

Illustrations:

tending to distribute the

DIPLOMACY

Concept:

Skill or tact in dealing with others while maintaining their goodwill.

Positively Directed:

- Can get things done without antagonism or hostility.
- Negotiates to achieve win–win solutions.
- Can gain the cooperation of others.

Negatively Directed:

- Can use too much time achieving harmonious relationships at the expense of other desired outcomes.
- May not stand up well to intimidation tactics.
- Can be a "con artist."

Indication:

The lower–case letters of a word or words become increasingly shorter. Diplomacy is also indicated when successive mounds in m's and n's become smaller and when the second letter of double l's and double t's are shorter than the first.

Illustrations:

smaller batters are better

DIRECTNESS

Concept:
The ability to come quickly to the point in thinking, speaking, writing and acting.

Positively Directed:
- Saves time by getting to the point.
- Focuses on the important things.
- Communications with others are often very clear.

Negatively Directed:
- Can injure relationships and the feelings of others when getting straight to the point.
- May miss out on some of the finer points of a problem or opportunity in the rush to get to the heart of a matter.
- Getting quickly to the point may not allow time to consider the ideas of others.

Indication:
An absence of approach strokes.

Illustrations:

there aren't any today

DOMINATING

Concept:
Through an act of will, ruling, directing or exercising control over the activities of others.

Positively Directed:
- Easily able to give orders and direct others.
- Able to assume a leadership position in a group.
- Requests are made in an authoritative way.

Negatively Directed:
- Can incur the resentment of others when taking charge.
- Can be demanding and brusque in social situations.
- Not usually a good team player.

Indication:
Thick, downward sloping t-bars.

Illustrations:

that isn't the

DOMINEERING

Concept:

Similar to dominating behaviour in that it is an act of will that rules, directs or exercises control over the activities of others but, in so doing, uses methods that would be generally characterized as tyrannical, overbearing, exploitative, etc.

Positively Directed:

- Easily able to give orders and direct others.
- Able to assume a leadership position in a group.
- Requests are made in an authoritative way.

Negatively Directed:

- Incurs the resentment and non-cooperation of others when taking charge.
- Little or no regard for the feelings or welfare of others.
- Appears "bossy" and overbearing.

Indication:

Downward sloping t–bars with pointed right end.

Illustrations:

this isnt either

ENTHUSIASM

Concept:
The pursuit of interests or goals with eagerness, fervour, zeal or passion.

Positively Directed:
- Contributes additional effort to job or task completion.
- Inspires others to increased confidence and effort.
- Adds an air of authority when communicating with others.

Negatively Directed:
- Could have overly optimistic or unrealistic expectations.
- If the energy expended is too great at the outset, it could be exhausted before the goal is reached.
- The "cheer-leader" personality could be a "turn off" for certain others.

Indication:
T–bars are longer than the distance between the feet (points of contact with the base line) of the t. When the bars are thick, the enthusiasm is strong; when they are long, it is enduring.

Illustrations:

the right attitude

EVASIVENESS

Concept:
Without telling a lie, the intentional avoidance of the truth by dodging, ducking or being vague, indirect or ambiguous.

Positively Directed:
- Can change subjects easily.
- Without lying, can escape embarrassing or negative moments.
- Can avoid taking a strong position on an issue.

Negatively Directed:
- Can leave others with a distorted picture of the truth.
- Difficult to know where one stands on an issue.
- Can undermine one's integrity.

Indication:
Hooks at the top of circle letters. They may be either a double hook or a single initial hook.

Illustrations:

have to ask now

FATALISM

Concept:
A resignation or an acceptance that circumstances or events are likely to be unfavourable.

Positively Directed:
- Willing to accept adversity.
- Doesn't waste time fighting what appears to be in- evitable.
- May make the best of negative situations and take them in stride.

Negatively Directed:
- Inclined to give up too easily.
- May avoid responsibility for making appropriate changes.
- May appear to back down in the face of adversity.

Indication:
Word endings that droop and fall below the base line.

Illustrations:

FRANKNESS

Concept:
Complete honesty without deception, secretiveness or evasiveness.

Positively Directed:
- Can usually be trusted to tell the truth.
- Willing to disclose feelings and thoughts.
- Openness inspires trust in others.

Negatively Directed:
- Openness and candor could be a handicap in certain discussions or negotiations.
- The tendency to verbalize every thought could lead to indiscretions.
- When pressed, not easily able to avoid taking a position or expressing an opinion.

Indication:
Circle letters that are clear of all hooks and loops.

Illustrations:

are what you eat

GENEROSITY

Concept:

The disposition to give freely to others without expectations of personal gain. Such giving could involve one's time, money or other resources.

Positively Directed:
- Contributes easily to the welfare of others.
- Inspires others to be cooperative and generous in return.
- Job completion is enhanced when extra effort is contributed.

Negatively Directed:
- A tendency to give away more than can be afforded.
- Giving too much can create dependency in others.
- Can be taken advantage of or create selfishness in others.

Indication:

Long final strokes at the end of words.

Illustrations:

what goes around

GOAL SETTING

Concept:
Determining the end toward which effort is directed.

Positively Directed:
- Higher goals stretch and develop talent.
- Higher goal setters are usually long range planners.
- Higher goal setters usually perform to higher standards.

Negatively Directed:
- When all goals are high, the individual may be impractical.
- When goals are too low, the individual is not likely developing or performing to potential.
- Low goal setters are more focused on the present and lack a future orientation.

Indication:
On the letter t, the higher the t-bar is on the t-stem, the higher the writer sets goals. High goals are set in the upper third of the t-stem. Practical goals are set in the middle third and low goals are set in the bottom third. T-bars set above the stem usually indicate a dreamer unless they are quite heavy and we also see some achievement traits. Then, we may have a visionary.

Illustrations:

distant   *practical*   *lowest*

High   **Practical**   **Low**

HUMOUR

Concept:

The ability to recognize, appreciate or express anything that is incongruous or funny.

Positively Directed:
- Adds to one's charm or appeal.
- Can relieve tension and lighten the burdens of life.
- Helps to maintain balance in one's life.

Negatively Directed:
- Can be expressed at the expense of others.
- Can be overdone and interfere with getting the job done.
- Can make light of situations that should be treated with more seriousness.

Indication:

Soft flourishes leading into a downstroke. They are most frequently found in capital M's and N's.

Illustrations:

HUMOUR, DRY

Concept:
Humour that is often expressed with little or no show of emotion and can sometimes be made at the expense of others.

Positively Directed:
- Adds to one's charm or appeal.
- Can relieve tension and lighten the burdens of life.
- Helps to maintain balance in one's life.

Negatively Directed:
- Can be expressed at the expense of others.
- Can be so subtle that others miss the point.
- Can make light of situations that should be treated more seriously.

Indication:
Almost the same as Humour except the initial curve is not flourished but smoothly curved before joining the downstroke.

Illustrations:

IDIOSYNCRASY

Concept:
A liking for the different and unusual. It can take the form of a distinguishing personal habit, quirk, peculiarity or mannerism.

Positively Directed:
- Looks for and often finds an unusual solution to a problem.
- Others remember the individual.
- Often adds some flair to a project or piece of work.

Negatively Directed:
- Could be more concerned with style than with content.
- Behavior could be distracting to others and interfere with work completion.
- Sometimes these people are not the best team players.

Indication:
Circles instead of dots over i's and j's.

Illustrations:

a little different

IMAGINATION

Concept:

The process of forming mental images of ideas and objects that are not present in physical reality.

Positively Directed:
- Frequently find novel or original solutions.
- Often very flexible and adaptable individuals.
- Generally make good team players.

Negatively Directed:
- Not usually good at working alone.
- Sometimes have more ideas than they can handle.
- Others don't always take these people seriously as they generate many ideas and tend to exaggerate.

Indication:

Loops. The larger the loops, the larger the imagination. Loops below the base line indicate material or practical imagination. Loops above the height of the lower–case letters indicate abstract or conceptual imagination.

Illustrations:

baby's body lay

Abstract   Material   Both

IMAGINATION, LATENT

Concept:
Sometimes, an individual with the ability to generate new ideas, fails to complete an idea or bring it into physical reality.

Positively Directed:
- Can be more suited to routine, repetitive tasks than creative ones.
- Can be better at executing the plan than creating it.
- Can be more disposed to following instructions without taking the time to question them.

Negatively Directed:
- Frequently misses the opportunity to achieve.
- May get frustrated by the lack of results.
- Others could see this person as lazy.

Indication:
Incomplete or open lower loops in the g, j, y or z.

Illustrations:

many great days

INDECISIVENESS

Concept:

The inability to arrive at a judgement, conclusion or decision.

Positively Directed:

- Waits for all possible input before acting.
- Decisions are well-researched, thought through and rarely made in haste.
- Some problems that originally seemed urgent can become less pressing if not acted upon.

Negatively Directed:

- While taking excessive time to decide, opportunities can be missed.
- Compromises achievement when slow to decide on goals and actions.
- Not usually able to take a firm stand.

Indication:

Found on final strokes with weak or feeble endings. Opposite of decisiveness, page 44.

Illustrations:

I can't decide

INDEPENDENT THINKING

Concept:
Making up one's own mind with little or no regard to what others are thinking or doing.

Positively Directed:
- Not easily influenced by peer pressure.
- Thinks for him/herself and doesn't need others to form own thoughts and judgments.
- Will challenge precedent, procedure and red tape.

Negatively Directed:
- Will sometimes overlook the legitimate input of others.
- May risk alienating others by not conforming to the group's norms of behavior.
- Not usually a good team player.

Indication:
T and d–stems are no taller than twice the height of the lower–case letters.

Illustrations:

I tend to disagree

INITIATIVE

Concept:
The capacity to begin thought or action without being directed to do so by others.

Positively Directed:
- Can easily identify opportunities to take action.
- Does not wait for or depend upon others to generate ideas or plans.
- A self–starter.

Negatively Directed:
- Will sometimes leave others behind.
- Sometimes not a good team player.
- This trait can be applied to negative activity as easily as positive activity.

Indication:
Following a downstroke to the base line, a break–away upstroke that moves sharply to the right. Often seen in the final stroke of a t or in the buckle of an h, k or p.

Illustrations:

to put that bet

INTUITIVENESS

Concept:
The ability to acquire knowledge or awareness of something without the conscious use of reason.

Positively Directed:
- Anticipates well and prepares for events.
- When information is distorted, can still make sound decisions.
- Good sense for the feelings and motives of others.

Negatively Directed:
- Can be used without regard to logic and reason.
- Other people may be reluctant to follow the leader who relies too heavily on intuition.
- Can be used for negative ends as well as for positive ones.

Indication:
Clear, decisive breaks between the letters within words, except for those immediately following capital letters.

Illustrations:

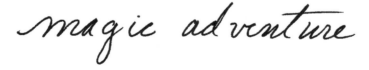

IRRITABILITY

Concept:
Easily prone to becoming annoyed, impatient, exasperated or angered.

Positively Directed:
- Can drive self to get the job done quickly.
- Works well at own pace and by oneself.
- Often a self–starter.

Negatively Directed:
- Feelings of frustration can disrupt composure.
- When annoyed, mistakes are more likely to happen.
- Not usually a good team player.

Indication:
I–dots and j–dots are formed like dashes or jabs and are usually positioned to the right of the stems. Also, t–bars on the right of and touching the stems. The heavier the stroke, the more intense the irritability and the longer it takes to recover from the feeling.

Illustrations:

joining the team

JEALOUSY

Concept:
A state of fear caused by a real or imagined risk of losing favour, approval or affection to another. Can be demonstrated by rivalry, suspicion, resentment or envy.

Positively Directed:
- Compels one to be competitive.
- Motivation to be popular.
- Drive towards achievement.

Negatively Directed:
- Can induce rivalry.
- Can breed suspicion.
- Can lead to unrealistic fear of others.

Indication:
Small, tight, initial loops that start with a flat-bottomed leftward loop. They appear most frequently on capital or small m's, n's and w's.

Illustrations:

Men and Women

LINE VALUE

Concept:
A sense of and appreciation for balance, proportion, perspective and symmetry.

Positively Directed:
- Can position things well against a background.
- Can achieve good balance and symmetry when arranging things.
- Good at arranging things in an appropriate order.

Negatively Directed:
- Becomes agitated when pictures are not properly balanced on a wall.
- Can get upset when clothes are not matched or co–ordinated.
- Might annoy others by rearranging things that they have arranged.

Indication:
Writing that is consistent, balanced, and graceful.

Illustrations:

As we agreed, effective June 1, 1991, this loan has been rescinded and replaced by a new loan in the amount of $20,000, payable over a 20-year term at the rate of 10.75 percent, fixed for five

LITERARY LEANINGS

Concept:

An aptitude for writing. It could be for poetry or prose. It could be as an author or editor. If indicated, but not strongly, the writer might be more inclined towards reading than writing.

Positively Directed:

- Appreciates good writing.
- Skillful communicator in written and spoken form.
- Fluent and skillful in choosing words.

Negatively Directed:

- May become discouraged if working or living in circumstances that do not support or encourage literary pursuits.
- Could apply talents to the "dark side" of the literary world.
- May discount the abilities of those who do not appreciate the same interests.

Indication:

Greek e's, delta d's or figure eights found typically in g's, f's or s's.

Illustrations:

read for gaining ideas

MANUAL DEXTERITY

Concept:
Skill or deftness in using the hands or body.

Positively Directed:
- Skillful in manually building and repairing.
- Generally good at mechanical, electrical, electronic and other pursuits involving motor skills.
- Expresses oneself creatively through the use of the body.

Negatively Directed:
- Can experience frustration if these skills are not put to use.
- Manual skills can be pursued at the expense of intellectual development.
- Runs the risk of being displaced by technology.

Indication:
Flat-topped structures. Most often found in r's, m's, n's and in connecting strokes.

Illustrations:

maker of more

NARROW–MINDEDNESS

Concept:
Holding narrow views or lacking breadth of ideas. Intolerance for ideas and practices that differ from one's own.

Positively Directed:
- Assists one in controlling impulsiveness.
- Can be selective in adopting new ideas.
- Steadfast and loyal to own ideas and practices.

Negatively Directed:
- Often misses the benefits of new and alternative ideas.
- Intolerant of differing viewpoints.
- Difficult to be empathetic, understanding or tolerant.

Indication:
Narrow or closed e's, as opposite to the wide or open e's that indicate broad–mindedness.

Illustrations:

doesn't need the tea

OPTIMISM

Concept:
A disposition to see the better side of situations and to expect that outcomes will be positive.

Positively Directed:
- Increases the energy that can be applied to activity.
- Helps to overcome adversity and disappointment.
- Contributes to belief in successful outcomes which enhances success.

Negatively Directed:
- May take problems too lightly and not address them appropriately.
- Overstating the brighter side of failure and adversity might annoy others.
- In the extreme, may result in an unrealistic or impractical outlook.

Indication:
The upward inclination of words, lines of writing and t–bars.

Illustrations:

this is up - beat

ORGANIZATIONAL ABILITY

Concept:

The ability to assemble and arrange ideas, items or events in logical order.

Positively Directed:
- Can easily bring parts together to form a whole.
- Contributes to efficiency.
- Brings structure and perspective to ideas, plans and events.

Negatively Directed:
- Risks spending too much time in the planning phase at the expense of execution.
- Can be applied to negative pursuits as well as to positive ones.
- When carried to extremes, can be annoying to others.

Indication:

Lower case f's are balanced. That is, the distance from the base line to the top of the upper loop is the same as the distance from the base line to the bottom of the lower loop. This is also indicated by clear delineation between the lines of writing, unlike confusion of interest, page 42.

Illustrations:

find for your friends

OSTENTATION

Concept:

Vain, pretentious or exaggerated display of wealth, luxury, skill, knowledge, etc. Intended to attract attention or admiration to oneself.

Positively Directed:

- Assists in promoting self.
- Stands out from the crowd.
- Can enhance creativity.

Negatively Directed:

- Often viewed as acting in poor taste.
- Can be perceived as showing off.
- This individuality can conflict with being a team player.

Indication:

Exaggerated flourishes and individualistic strokes.

Illustrations:

PERSISTENCE

Concept:
The relentless pursuit of a goal in the face of setbacks. The drive to start over or to try again.

Positively Directed:
- Finds creative ways of overcoming obstacles and barriers.
- Doesn't give up or back down.
- Isn't easily deterred by opposition or difficulty.

Negatively Directed:
- May not know when to back away or give up.
- May not easily give up a negative habit.
- May push subordinates, teammates or others too much.

Indication:
When an up-stroke moves to the left of the preceding down-stroke, forms a loop and then travels across itself as it proceeds onward, to the right. This loop is most often found in t's and f's.

Illustrations:

try for first & try for

PESSIMISM

Concept:
A disposition to see the worst side of situations and to expect that outcomes will be negative.

Positively Directed:
- Can quickly see the weak side of a situation.
- Would tend to think through all of the aspects of a situation before taking action.
- Could bring balance to a group of optimists.

Negatively Directed:
- Focus on the downside diminishes effort to achieve.
- The view of the future is negative and discouraging.
- A negative view could cause others to become discouraged.

Indication:
The downward inclination of words and lines of writing.

Illustrations:

this is down - beat writing

PHYSICAL–MINDEDNESS

Concept:
A desire to engage in physical activity such as athletics, dance or other forms of muscular movement. This desire can still exist when the person is physically incapable of such activity.

Positively Directed:
- Can contribute to physical fitness.
- Useful when physical work needs to be done.
- Can more easily lead by example.

Negatively Directed:
- Little patience for sitting still.
- Can lead to frustration if the physical ability is not commensurate with the desire, e.g. physical handicap.
- May have a tendency to act before an appropriate amount of thought.

Indication:
Loops in lower-case p's. The larger the loops, the stronger the desire for muscular movement.

Illustrations:

put the pole upon the

POSITIVENESS

Concept:
The strong affirmation of a decision or opinion that leaves no doubt or question as to one's position.

Positively Directed:
- Positions are stated clearly and confidently.
- Stands firm and is not easily moved from positions.
- Little time is wasted second-guessing.

Negatively Directed:
- Firmly expressed positions can discourage others from expressing alternative points of view.
- Can be inflexible when accommodating change.
- Changing one's mind or position is not done easily.

Indication:
Downstrokes that fall directly to the base line and are followed by a lift of the pen.

Illustrations:

put it around him

PRECISION, PHYSICAL

Concept:
The disposition to perform physical operations with exactness and accuracy.

Positively Directed:
- Outputs are accurate.
- Good sense of rhythm and timing.
- Good attention to detail.

Negatively Directed:
- Could get too involved in details and miss seeing the larger picture.
- Others may be annoyed by fastidiousness
- May spend too much time pursuing perfection.

Indication:
The absence of a loop below the base line on a lower-case p. The downstroke below the base line is retraced by the upstroke.

Illustrations:

placed precisely as planned

PRIDE

Concept:
A sense of self–respect, personal dignity and satisfaction in one's accomplishments. The concept includes a healthy desire for the approval of others.

Positively Directed:
- Dress, grooming and personal habits are well attended to.
- Doing a job well is important.
- Proper protocol is usually valued and followed.

Negatively Directed:
- Runs the risk of being unduly influenced by the approval of others.
- May emphasize the "package" at the expense of the contents.
- Interest in doing a job well can be applied to negative pursuits as well as to positive ones.

Indication:
T–stems and d–stems are between two and two and one half times the height of the lower-case letters.

Illustrations:

treading water and wait.

PROCRASTINATION

Concept:
The habit of delaying action to the point of incurring risks such as missed deadlines or incomplete projects.

Positively Directed:
- More delay can mean more preparation and consideration.
- Sometimes, delay proves that the intended action was never necessary.
- Putting things off until tomorrow gives one more time to enjoy today.

Negatively Directed:
- Can jeopardize work completion.
- Can frustrate others.
- Rushing to complete things at the last minute risks missing deadlines and doing poor quality work.

Indication:
T–bars, i–dots and j–dots falling on the left of their respective stems. They may or may not be touching the stems.

Illustrations:

is not joining it

REGRESSION

Concept:
A focus or fixation on the past when times may have been happier or more secure.

Positively Directed:
- Can appear optimistic when there is little reason for it.
- Happy memories can have a sustaining power.
- May be encouraging to others when circumstances are grim.

Negatively Directed:
- Living in the past may not be realistic.
- Can lead to pessimism about the present and future.
- May not see some of the benefits and opportunities of the present or future.

Indication:
Incomplete lower loops that begin with a downstroke, move to the left (the past) and do not return upward to the base line.

Illustrations:

living   every   yesterday

REJECTION

Concept:
Because of some past emotional injury, disappointment or disillusionment, an individual no longer accepts a previously loved or highly valued person, belief or ambition. The emotional injury could also include being rejected.

Positively Directed:
- May keep some unpleasant memories hidden.
- May dissolve an unpleasant relationship.
- May change beliefs or ambitions to happier ones.

Negatively Directed:
- May not be facing reality.
- Can lead to resentment, anger, hatred and other negative feelings that can compromise well being.
- May reject people, beliefs, etc. that are contrary to own best interests.

Indication:
The lower loops of y's, g's, j's and z's are reversed and have upstrokes that are mostly on the right side of the downstroke.

Illustrations:

get away and stay

REPRESSION

Concept:

A defense mechanism whereby an individual denies feelings, thoughts or events to the extent that they are pushed out of conscious memory and into the unconscious mind where the individual becomes unaware of their existence and influence.

Positively Directed:

- In the short run, can protect from unpleasant memories.
- A useful survival mechanism.
- Maintains the ego by temporarily reducing or eliminating feelings of guilt, shame or self–depreciation.

Negatively Directed:

- Sooner or later, built–up tension is released, some- times explosively.
- Reduces analytical ability.
- Inhibits free self–expression.

Indication:

Letters are squeezed, causing upstrokes to retrace downstrokes in m's, n's, h's and r's. There must be a definite "pinched" look to these letters.

Illustrations:

cannot remember how

RESENTMENT

Concept:
A feeling of hurt or of being taken advantage of because of some real or imagined imposition, interference, criticism, insult or injustice.

Positively Directed:
- Can alert the individual to possible transgressions.
- Reduces the likelihood of being taken advantage of.
- Situations are approached with a degree of skepticism.

Negatively Directed:
- Can lead to too much suspicion and distrust of others.
- Is difficult to forgive and forget transgressions.
- Not likely a good team player.

Indication:
Straight, rigid approach strokes that start at or below the base line.

Illustrations:

letting go is tough

RESPONSIBILITY, DESIRE FOR

Concept:
A desire to improve self–image or to be important to others by taking on tasks or positions of responsibility.

Positively Directed:
- Interested in advancement.
- Can be depended upon to do at least a fair share of the work.
- Looks for what needs to be done.

Negatively Directed:
- Could take on more than can handle.
- Could have this desire for reasons such as jealousy, fear of not being liked, fear of rivalry.
- May take on things that can and should be done by others.

Indication:
Large, initial loops that start with a move to the left. They appear most frequently on capital or small m's, n's and w's. The desire for an important self-image becomes greater as these loops become larger.

Illustrations:

Make My Mom Mad

RETICENCE

Concept:
An inclination to be silent or reserved in conversation. The opposite of talkative.

Positively Directed:
- Contributes to being a good listener.
- Could be a good quality for a negotiator.
- In conflict situations, silence could be the appropriate response.

Negatively Directed:
- May have some difficulty making friends.
- May hesitate to express ideas and feelings that are important for others or for the occasion.
- Others may discount or overlook the quiet individual.

Indication:
Closed circle letters.

Illustrations:

look and don't talk

SARCASM

Concept:
Humorous statements with a cruel edge that are intended to reduce the self–respect of the receiver. They employ language that can be termed ironic, scornful, bitter, caustic, stinging, contemptuous, taunting, biting, etc.

Positively Directed:
- Can be an effective tactic for keeping an adversary "off balance."
- Can put another "on the defensive."
- Can keep people from getting too close.

Negatively Directed:
- Reduces one's ability to make and keep friends.
- Invites retaliation which may shift attention from the main point of a discussion.
- Creates unnecessary animosity and tension.

Indication:
T–bars that progressively narrow to a point on the right side.

Illustrations:

butt of that tale

SECRETIVENESS

Concept:
The inclination to conceal thoughts, feelings and knowledge from others.

Positively Directed:
- Can be trusted to keep a matter confidential.
- Can be effective when guardedness is called for.
- Will not likely tell others more than they need to know.

Negatively Directed:
- Won't easily share complete information with others.
- Risks the perception of being stingy and not a team player.
- May inhibit intimacy with others.

Indication:
A loop on the interior, right side of lower case circle letters.

Illustrations:

don't talk too often

SELECTIVITY

Concept:
The inclination to choose a narrow range of experiences, interests and friends. Choices may be based on rather limited criteria or particular standards.

Positively Directed:
- Exercises care when choosing friends and experiences.
- Friends are not many but they are usually close and trusted.
- Inclined to be a specialist.

Negatively Directed:
- May have narrow range of experience.
- Usually not a generalist.
- Not likely to have many close friends.

Indication:
Slender lower loops in g's, j's, y's and z's.

Illustrations:

may give money away

SELF–CASTIGATION

Concept:
The excessive rebuking, chastising, criticizing or punishing of oneself.

Positively Directed:
- Considers oneself first when looking to assign blame.
- Would be willing to accept blame for the sake of peace.
- Likely the last one to point the finger at another.

Negatively Directed:
- Too hard on oneself.
- Takes on guilt feeling when not guilty.
- Overindulges in self–blame and guilt feeling at the expense of taking positive corrective action.

Indication:
When t–stems are completed, the pen stays on the paper and crosses the stem to form the bar by making a stroke upward and to the left.

Illustrations:

dont want guilt

SELF–CONSCIOUSNESS

Concept:
An undue amount of thought directed toward how others might assess one's appearance or behavior.

Positively Directed:
- Contributes to a presentable appearance.
- Keeps an individual on his/her best behavior.
- Prevents one from attracting an undue amount of attention.

Negatively Directed:
- Can inhibit one from free expression.
- Can prevent an individual from asserting him/herself.
- Focus on the self lessens attention to others.

Indication:
The final mound on m's or n's is higher than the rest of the letter. In the case of double l's and double t's, the second one is higher than the first.

Illustrations:

May not be going

SELF–DECEIT

Concept:
Unintentionally deluding oneself. An unconscious tendency to avoid facing unpleasantness.

Positively Directed:
- Helps to overcome unhappiness.
- Sees situations as brighter than they might really be.
- Puts a more positive light on life by avoiding unpleasantness.

Negatively Directed:
- Avoids dealing with problems.
- Provides excuses rather than solutions.
- Can form conclusions without considering all of the facts.

Indication:
A loop on the interior, left side of lower case circle letters.

Illustrations:

who is fooling around

SELF–ESTEEM

Concept:
The good opinion or value that one has of oneself. Developed initially through the love and support of parents and others and, later in life, by achievement and successful experiences.

Positively Directed:
- Fosters a liking and respect for oneself.
- Develops confidence in one's abilities.
- Moves one to take risks.

Negatively Directed:
- May not know limitations and exceed them.
- Could result in egocentricity.
- Can be a quality that supports the criminal as well as the honest person.

Indication:
Capital letters are approximately two and one half to four times the height of the lower–case letters.

Illustrations:

My Name is Brian

SELF–RELIANCE

Concept:
A desire to depend on one's own abilities and resources to achieve one's goals.

Positively Directed:
- Develops confidence in one's abilities and resources.
- Minimizes the amount of help required from others.
- Facilitates learning by doing.

Negatively Directed:
- Risks missing out on learning from other people's ideas and abilities.
- Tends not to ask for help when required.
- Tends not to accept help when offered.

Indication:
Underlining of one's signature.

Illustrations:

Andy Pendant

SENSITIVENESS TO CRITICISM

Concept:
A disposition to feeling hurt or persecuted when the object of criticism.

Positively Directed:
- Increases attention to the suggestions, criticisms and judgments of others.
- Provides motivation to work to a high standard so as to avoid negative criticism.
- Can be more responsive to the suggestions and preferences of customers and others.

Negatively Directed:
- Too easily hurt and swayed by the words of others.
- Avoids taking risks for fear of censure.
- May not be easily supervised.

Indication:
T–stems and d–stems are looped.

Illustrations:

don't dare do it

STUBBORNNESS

Concept:

Persistence in holding on to opinions, ideas or positions when the facts establish that doing so is not reasonable.

Positively Directed:

- Can be a good defense in the face of aggression.
- Not admitting mistakes can be an effective negotiating tactic.
- Adds persuasiveness when bluffing.

Negatively Directed:

- Liable to act contrary to reason.
- Reduces the ability to be flexible and respond appropriately to necessary change.
- Risks alienating others.

Indication:

Inverted v–shaped t and d–stems with the downstroke forming an obtuse angle with the base line.

Illustrations:

don't dare do it

TALKATIVENESS

Concept:
The inclination to talk more than most people. This trait must be motivated by a desire to communicate ideas and not just talk to relieve tension or to be sociable.

Positively Directed:
- Can easily carry his/her end of the conversation.
- Finds it easy to speak up and express points of view and opinions.
- Contributes to sociability.

Negatively Directed:
- Can become tiring for others.
- Can interfere with effective listening.
- Can impede learning.

Indication:
Circle letters that are open at the top.

Illustrations:

don't open that door

TEMPER

Concept:
The disposition to become angry.

Positively Directed:
- Can be an effective defense against aggression.
- Can be an effective negotiating tactic.
- Can help to emphasize a point of discussion.

Negatively Directed:
- Can interfere with clear thinking.
- Can be disruptive to relationships.
- Can lose friends and alienate others.

Indication:
A short initial stroke followed by an abrupt change in direction. Also, a fairly heavy t-bar to the right of the t-stem (not touching it).

Illustrations:

Had not thought

TENACITY

Concept:
The proclivity to hold on firmly and to not easily let go of ideas, possessions or beliefs.

Positively Directed:
- Keeps that which is achieved.
- Doesn't easily give up or let things slip away.
- Holds on in order to see a task completed.

Negatively Directed:
- Doesn't know when to quit, even when the battle is over.
- May not easily let go of emotional baggage, e.g. anger, hatred, resentment.
- Not easily able to change ways of behaving.

Indication:
Hooks at the end of t–bars or final strokes.

Illustrations:

don't let go of it

VANITY

Concept:
Excessively high opinion of one's appearance, achievements or oneself. Inclined to be easily moved by the opinions and preferences of others.

Positively Directed:
- Achievement can be motivated by the approval of others.
- Behavior is frequently directed to achieve the approval of others.
- The high opinion of oneself can lead to the undertaking of challenging goals.

Negatively Directed:
- Can be manipulated by others.
- The estimate of one's own aptitudes and abilities might exceed reality.
- Finds it difficult to admit errors and shortcomings.

Indication:
The height of t-stems and d-stems exceed two and one half times the height of the lower-case letters.

Illustrations:

don't do as others direct

VARIETY, DESIRE FOR

Concept:
An inclination towards varied experiences, ideas, possessions and friends, and away from sameness and routine.

Positively Directed:
- Adaptable and can handle a wide range of assignments, circumstances, people, challenges, etc.
- Brings flexibility to a job and to other aspects of life.
- Likes to keep busy.

Negatively Directed:
- May not finish a task before moving on to a new one.
- Not good at routine.
- Generally not a specialist.

Indication:
Found in wide lower loops of y's, g's and q's. The wider the loop, the more the individual desires variety.

Illustrations:

going away today

WILLPOWER

Concept:

The ability to direct one's mind, emotions or actions consciously, deliberately and with a sense of purpose.

Positively Directed:

- Likely to be a goal setter.
- Usually self–disciplined.
- Likely a self–starter.

Negatively Directed:

- It can be difficult to change such an individual's mind.
- When goals are different than the team's, may not be a good team player.
- May be difficult to supervise.

Indication:

Indicated by t–bars that are thicker than the rest of the writing. The thicker the t–bar, the stronger the willpower.

Illustrations:

that is not the top

WORRY

Concept:
A feeling of anxiety, excessive concern or apprehension about an event or outcome.

Positively Directed:
- Leads to conscientiousness and concern.
- Prepares one for the worst.
- Can anticipate problems before they arise.

Negatively Directed:
- Wastes time and energy fretting about things that never happen.
- Tends to focus the mind on the negative side of life.
- Can cause dis-ease and illness.

Indication:
Undersided loops in m's, n's and lower–case h's that are formed when the upstroke rises on the left side of the down-stroke. The loop rests on or near the base line and looks like an inverted e.

Illustrations:

many miserable men

YIELDINGNESS

Concept:

The disposition to give way to others.

Positively Directed:

- Easily steps aside to accommodate the wishes of others.
- Avoids conflict.
- Enjoys team play and cooperating with others.

Negatively Directed:

- Can be taken advantage of.
- Can lack assertiveness.
- Can be persuaded to put aside own goals or agenda in favor of other people's.

Indication:

Found in strokes that are rounded or flattened. Most prevalent in lower-case s's and p's.

Illustrations:

positive push and pull

6

PRODUCING AN ANALYSIS

By now you will have learned how to examine handwriting to develop insights into the emotions, certain elements of thinking and 75 other aspects of personality. Now comes the challenge of putting it all together in an organized fashion so that you can communicate a coherent analysis.

There are many ways you can do this and the way you select should depend upon your purpose. For example, if your purpose is personnel selection, you might want to organize traits in a way that matches job criteria or incumbent specifications, or both. If your purpose is career guidance, you might want to emphasize specific occupational aptitudes and personality traits that contribute to achievement.

To illustrate what I mean, I have developed a worksheet that is based upon the lessons of the foregoing chapters and is designed to deliver a general analysis. I invite you to try it, challenge it and build some worksheets of your own.

Keep in mind that this is only one way of organizing information for an analysis. You might elect to use other categories for your purposes. You might feel that some of the traits I have included don't belong or that you would like to add others. The choices are yours but I do want to make two points: one, you should use some type of worksheet to organize your information and help communicate your analysis; and two, keeping your purpose in mind, you can then design your worksheet to include whichever traits and information that are applicable to achieving your purpose.

HANDWRITING ANALYSIS WORKSHEET

Guidelines:

100 consecutive strokes should be measured for slant, taken from somewhere near the middle of your sample. If you do less than this number, work out the percentages so that your total equals 100 percent.

Most people's slant falls into one or two principal areas with scatterings in one or two others. A typical profile might look like: 70% responsive, 25% mildly responsive and 5% highly responsive.

For depth, select a three, five or ten–point scale, then, based on your estimate of how heavy the writing is, record your estimate. For example, if you select a five–point scale, you might estimate that a heavier than average script is about a four.

The four thinking styles should also total 100 percent. Most people will have one dominant style and possibly one or two others. A typical score might be 85% investigative and 15% comprehensive.

For analytical ability, fluidity of thought, intellectual efficiency and all the other traits that follow, use the same point scale that you used for depth. In selecting points on this scale, take into account each trait's **intensity** and **frequency**.

Intensity is the degree of strength the trait manifests. If it is extremely strong, you might give it a 5; if it is quite weak, you might assign a 1. Frequency considers the number of times the trait appeared out of all the times that it could have appeared. So, if it appears at every opportunity, give it a 5; if it appears rarely, you might give it a 1. A blend of intensity and frequency is what gives you your evaluation, e.g. an intensity of 5 and a frequency of 1 might lead you to a score of 3 on a particular trait.

A. EMOTIONS

1—Extreme Withdrawal   _____
2—Withdrawal   _____
3—Mildly Responsive   _____   Depth ____
4—Responsive   _____
5—Highly Responsive   _____
          Total   100%

B. THINKING

Comprehensive   _____
Cumulative   _____   Analytical Ability ____
Exploratory   _____   Fluidity of Thought ____
Investigative   _____   Intellectual Efficiency ____
          Total   100%

C. POTENTIAL FOR ACHIEVEMENT

Supportive Traits

Acquisitiveness _____
Aggressiveness _____
Broad–Mindedness _____
Change, Desire for _____
Concentration _____
Decisiveness _____
Detail, Attention to _____
Determination _____
Directness _____
Dominating _____
Enthusiasm _____
High Goals _____
Imagination _____
Initiative _____
Intuitiveness _____
Literary Leanings _____
Optimism _____
Organizational Ability _____
Persistence _____
Positiveness _____
Precision _____
Pride _____
Responsibility, Desire for _____
Self–Esteem _____
Self–Reliance _____
Tenacity _____
Variety, Desire for _____
Willpower _____

Reductive Traits

Caution _____
Confusion of Interests _____
Detail, Inattention to _____
Imagination, Latent _____
Indecisiveness _____
Low Goals _____
Narrow-Mindedness _____
Pessimism _____
Procrastination _____
Regression _____
Worry _____
Yieldingness _____

D. SOCIABILITY

Supportive Traits		**Reductive Traits**	
Dignity	_____	Argumentativeness	_____
Diplomacy	_____	Clannishness	_____
Frankness	_____	Deceit	_____
Generosity	_____	Domineering	_____
Humor,	_____	Evasiveness	_____
Humor, Dry	_____	Idiosyncrasy	_____
Imagination	_____	Impatience	_____
Intuitiveness	_____	Irritability	_____
Optimism	_____	Jealousy	_____
Physical–Mindedness	_____	Ostentation	_____
Pride	_____	Rejection	_____
Self–Esteem	_____	Resentment	_____
Self–Reliance	_____	Reticence	_____
Sensuousness	_____	Sarcasm	_____
Talkativeness	_____	Selectivity	_____
Variety, Desire for	_____	Self–Consciousness	_____
		Temper	_____

E. INTEGRITY

Supportive Traits		**Reductive Traits**	
Broad–Mindedness	____	Attention, Desire for	____
Caution	____	Deceit	____
Determination	____	Domineering	____
Dignity	____	Evasiveness	____
Directness	____	Jealousy	____
Frankness	____	Narrow-Mindedness	____
Generosity	____	Procrastination	____
Goals, High	____	Secretiveness	____
Persistence	____	Self–deceit	____
Pride	____	Vanity	____
Responsibility, Desire for	____	Will Power, weak	____
		Yieldingness	____

7

EMOTIONAL INTELLIGENCE

—

There is a large body of research that shows Emotional Intelligence is about three times more important to success in life, and in the workplace, than Cognitive Intelligence or IQ. This helps to explain why some very bright people often do dumb things or how it is that those with superior IQs often end up working for those with average IQs.

About 23 years ago, Dr. Reuven BarOn started his research on Emotional Intelligence and began pursuing an idea for an instrument to measure it. Over the years he fine-tuned and developed this instrument, norming it on well over 30,000 people in eight different countries. Today, the BarOn EQ-i is probably the world's foremost scientifically developed and validated measure of Emotional Intelligence. EQ-i stands for Emotional Quotient Inventory.

The world-wide distribution rights for the BarOn EQ-i are held by Multi-Health Systems Inc., a Toronto-based firm, owned and operated by Dr. Steven J. Stein, that publishes and distributes professional assessment materials. About five years ago, I attended one of their training programmes and became certified to administer and interpret the EQ-i.

Combining the EQ-i and handwriting analysis can be very powerful in personal coaching, employee selection, training needs assessment, outplacement counselling, career planning and team building. Unlike IQ which levels out in the teen years, EQ can grow and develop at almost any age.

This chapter shows you how handwriting analysis can go part way in identifying the elements that make up Dr. BarOn's concept of emotional intelligence. To my knowledge, there is no research that has specifically correlated handwriting strokes with emotional intelligence. The research that I am basing my conclusions on is that which has been done to correlate certain strokes in the handwriting with certain personality traits that are similar to the elements of the EQ-i.

On the one hand, handwriting analysis will not give you a validated emotional intelligence score and compare your score with that of thousands of others. The BarOn EQ-i will do this and, at the moment, is a much superior tool in this regard.

On the other hand, handwriting analysis can do much to show you the degree to which you possess the personality traits that are consistent with emotional intelligence. As well, it can provide you with much ammunition for developing and implementing strategies for improvement. It is reassuring to know that emotional intelligence is growable and you can make great strides in many of the components.

The EQ-i has fifteen *content subscales* that make up five *composite scales*. The fifteen subscales are numbered below under their respective composite scales (bold type). The official BarOn EQ-i definition has been provided for each.

Intrapersonal:

1. Emotional Self-Awareness—The ability to recognize and understand one's feelings and emotions, differentiate between them, know what caused them and why.
2. Assertiveness—The ability to express feelings, beliefs, and thoughts and defend one's rights in a non-destructive way.
3. Self-Regard—The ability to look at and understand oneself, respect and accept oneself, accepting one's perceived positive and negative aspects as well as one's limitations and possibilities.
4. Self-Actualization—The ability to realize one's potential capacities.
5. Independence—The ability to be self-reliant and self-directed in one's thinking and actions, and to be free of emotional dependency; these people may ask for and consider the advice of

others, but they rarely depend on others to make important decisions or do things for them.

Interpersonal:

1. Interpersonal Relationship—The ability to establish and maintain mutually satisfying relationships that are characterized by intimacy and by giving and receiving affection.
2. Empathy—The ability to be attentive to, to understand, and to appreciate the feelings of others... it is being able to "emotionally read" other people.
3. Social Responsibility—The ability to demonstrate oneself as a co-operative, contributing, and constructive member of one's social group.

Adaptability:

1. Problem Solving—The ability to identify and define problems as well as to generate and implement potentially effective solutions.
2. Reality Testing—The ability to assess the correspondence between what is experienced (the subjective) and what in reality exists (the objective).
3. Flexibility—The ability to adjust one's emotions, thoughts and behaviour to changing situations and conditions.

Stress Management:

1. Stress Tolerance—The ability to withstand adverse events and stressful situations without falling apart by actively and confidently coping with stress.

2. Impulse Control—The ability to resist or delay an impulse, drive or temptation to act.

General Mood:
1. Happiness—The ability to feel satisfied with one's life, to enjoy oneself and others, and to have fun.
2. Optimism—The ability to look at the brighter side of life and to maintain a positive attitude, even in the face of adversity.

On the next page, you will find a little worksheet that displays the fifteen subscales. For each of these subscales, there are a few personality traits which, taken together, make up a good deal of the meaning of the subscale. The handwriting strokes that indicate these traits are all in this book and the numbers you see beside the traits are the page numbers where the traits can be found.

Please realize that this is not a comprehensive nor scientifically validated list but one that was developed, for the most part, by a few colleagues (to whom I am most grateful) who gathered for a meeting of the Ontario Chapter of the International Graphoanalysis Society. Although this exercise may not be scientifically validated, it is based on some science and it yields a respectable indication of a writer's emotional intelligence. Certainly, it would give most of us a starting point if we wanted to develop our EI. And, that's the whole object of this chapter.

So, now the idea is to get a sample of writing that you wish to analyze for emotional intelligence and, on the lines, either check off the traits that you can identify in the sample or, better yet, place a value for any traits that you identify. A description of how you can assign a value is found in the guidelines, on page 116.

WORKSHEET

Intrapersonal:

1. Emotional— Self-Awareness	Analytical ability, 32	_____
	Intuitiveness, 71	_____
	Investigative Thinking, 30	_____
2. Assertiveness—	Positiveness, 84	_____
	Frankness, 60	_____
	Talkativeness, 104	_____
	Defiance, 49	_____
	Aggressiveness, 38	_____
	Argumentativeness, 39	_____
	Diplomacy, 53	_____
	Initiative, 70	_____
	Depth, 25	_____
	Directness, 54	_____
	Seeks Responsibility, 92	_____
3. Self-Regard	Self-Esteem, 100	_____
	Dignity, 52	_____
4. Self-Actualization	Depth, 25	_____
	Enthusiasm, 57	_____
	Willpower, 109	_____
	Persistence, 81	_____
	Initiative, 70	_____
	High Goals, 62	_____
	Aggressiveness, 38	_____
	Tenacity, 106	_____
	Determination, 51	_____

5. Independence | Self-Reliance, 101 | ____
Independent Thinking, 69 | ____
Humour, 63 | ____
Positiveness, 84 | ____
High Goals, 62 | ____

Interpersonal:

1. Interpersonal
   Relationship

Humour, 63 ____
Uniform Slant, 24 ____
Sensitivity to Criticism, 102 ____
Broad-Mindedness, 41 ____
Generosity, 61 ____
Intuitiveness, 71 ____
Diplomacy, 53 ____

2. Social
   Responsibility

Rightward Slant, 24 ____
Generosity, 61 ____
Depth, 25 ____
Material Imagination, 66 ____

3. Empathy

Intuitiveness, 71 ____
Rightward Slant, 24 ____
Broad-Mindedness, 41 ____
Depth, 25 ____

Adaptability:

1. Problem Solving

Analytical Ability, 32 _____
Directness, 54 _____
Caution, 42 _____
Investigative Thinking, 30 _____
Organization Ability, 79 _____
Attention to Detail, 40 _____
Cumulative Thinking, 29 _____
Imagination, 66 _____
Diplomacy, 53 _____
Intuitiveness, 71 _____
Fluidity of Thought, 33 _____
Broad-Mindedness, 41 _____
Aggressiveness, 38 _____
Initiative, 70 _____

2. Reality Testing

Writing above the Baseline _____
An Absence of:
Vanity, 107 _____
Rejection, 89 _____
Dreamer, 62 _____
Confusion of Interest, 46 _____
Self-Deceit, 99 _____
Overblown Imagination, 66
Signature vs. Text
Discrepancies, 15 _____

3. Flexibility

Consistent Slant, 24 _____
Broad-Mindedness, 41 _____
Fluidity of Thought, 33 _____

Stress Management:

1. Stress tolerance

    Objective Slant, 24 _____
    Humour, 63 _____
    Depth, 25 _____

2. Impulse Control

    Vertical Slant, 24 _____
    Dignity, 52 _____
    Diplomacy, 53 _____
    Humour, 63 _____

General Mood:

1. Happiness

    Enthusiasm, 57 _____
    Lack of Deceit, 47 _____
    Humour, 63 _____
    Optimism, 78 _____

2. Optimism

    Optimism, 78 _____
    Enthusiasm, 57 _____
    Diplomacy, 53 _____

8

RELATIONSHIPS AND COMPATIBILITY

—

With the professional expertise of psychotherapists, marriage counselors and others, what exactly is the role of a handwriting analyst when it comes to dealing with relationships and compatibility?

Well, I believe there is a niche where an handwriting analyst can be helpful. As I see it, the psychotherapists and such can provide wise counsel about how two people might accommodate their differences. What I believe a handwriting analyst can do is identify many of those differences and provide some insight into the degree to which they exist. After that, the professionals can provide their advice and the parties concerned can then decide what they intend to do about it, if anything.

In a nutshell, I believe that nearly any two people can be compatible if they really want to be. Granted, the more differences they have, the tougher it is. But, the formula is really quite simple: The couple must 1) identify what their differences are, 2) learn not to fear these differences, and 3) learn to accommodate them. The second and third are the challenging ones and this is where the professionals can be useful. Identifying the differences is where the handwriting analyst can make a contribution.

This Chapter then, has a fairly straight-forward mission: From the cursive script of two individuals, it will help the reader identify differences in over 80 personality traits and it will then provide some insight into the degree of difference that may exist for each of these traits. Once the differences and the degrees of difference are identified, the readers are off on their own adventure, and I wish them many fulfilling lessons and a happy result.

So, here's how it works: First, we need a sample of each party's handwriting. To get proper samples, follow the instructions on page 14. Next, use the Compatibility Analysis Worksheet from page 139. You will notice that the worksheet lists all of the traits that are treated in this book. There is a column to record the value of each of the traits, for each of the two parties. The third column is to record the degree of difference on each trait, between the two parties.

For the first and second columns, you can use a three, five, ten or any point scale you like to record the value of each trait. I suggest that a five point scale will do the job without getting too complicated. Remember also to take **intensity** and **frequency** into account. These considerations are explained in the worksheet guidelines, on page 116.

So, in evaluating both intensity and frequency, we make a decision on each trait. As you can see, this isn't an exact science and a good deal of judgment is required. For this exercise, don't worry too much that your evaluations of trait value may not be "bang on." Worry more that they be consistent. That is, be as consistent as you can be for the two samples involved. If you call a trait a 4 for one person's writing, call it a 4 for the next person who, in your judgment, has about the same amount of intensity and frequency on that trait.

To illustrate how to use the worksheet, I have used a shortened example worksheet that you can see on page 136. I have used two short samples of handwriting from two people referred to as **Person A** and **Person B**. On the example worksheet, values have been assigned to the emotions, thinking and the first seven traits from the worksheet.

Person A:

I am submitting a sample of ...
to be analyzed by a graphoa...
Recently, I have learned more ...
graphoanalysis and find the ...
intriguing and very accurate...
because of this, that I see ...
an excellent opportunity to ...
handwriting analyzed in orde...
.... about ...

Person B:

Here is a sample of my
handwriting. Please
tell me if there is
any chance that I
would be able to
live in harmony with
the person who wrote
sample A.

COMPATIBILITY ANALYSIS WORKSHEET

Trait	First Person	Second Person	Difference
Extreme Withdrawal	0	0	0
Withdrawal	0	0	0
Mildly Responsive	0	0	0
Moderately Responsive	0	0	0
Highly Responsive	5	5	0
Depth	3	4	1
Cumulative Thinking	0	0	0
Comprehensive Thin'g	1	0	1
Investigative Thinking	4	5	1
Exploratory Thinking	0	0	0
Analytical Ability	2	5	3*
Fluidity of Thought	0	2	2
Thinking Efficiency	3	4	1
Acquisitiveness	0	5	5*
Aggressiveness	0	0	0
Argumentativeness	0	0	0
Attention, Desire for	1	0	1
Broad-Mindedness	1	1	0
Caution	N/A	1	?
Change, Desire for	3	2	1

* These two items probably warrant some discussion.

By now, you probably have the idea and can begin to do your own Compatibility Analysis using the blank worksheet that follows. You may want to photocopy the worksheet each time you do an analysis, so please feel free to do so as many times as you like.

Now, just before you begin, a couple of reminders: First, Don't take this too seriously. It takes years of study and practice to become a good handwriting analyst and you are not going to become one overnight. What this exercise can do for you is identify areas that can invite discussion between two people who are interested in being compatible. Don't get into arguments over whether a trait's value should be 3 or 4. Just be flexible and pursue those discussions where there appear to be major differences. Go into the discussion with the attitude that minor differences may not be worth any discussion and those that appear to be major are worth talking about, first to verify that they do exist and then to determine what you will do about them, if anything.

Second, remember from page 17, no single handwriting stroke interpretation or personality trait stands alone. This means that the interpretation of any single stroke in a writing sample must take into account all other related strokes from the same sample. The competent analyst will usually find evidence in the sample that will either support or reduce the meaning of any single stroke. This must be taken into account if the analysis is to be accurate.

My caution, then, is to remember that this chapter is not designed to teach you how to be a professional counselor. Its mission is simply to help you identify those areas of personality where two people may have differences that are worthwhile knowing about so they can choose to discuss them or not and then take steps to accommodate them, or not.

Finally, here are a few personal observations about the compatibility of humans:

- If you think you can change other people, you are probably better off trying to push string uphill or nail Jell-O to the wall. It very seldom works.

- People we care about often reflect much of ourselves back to us. If we don't like what we see in the mirror, it's pointless to try and rearrange the image in the mirror. Instead, the change process most often begins with ourselves.
- If we want someone to understand us, it generally works better if we make an effort to understand them first.
- If we can keep quiet and really listen to others, we have a much better chance of understanding them.
- Strangely, if we are looking to get something, we can often accelerate the process by being a giver first.

That's generally how it works and yes, there's a few exceptions to each of these ideas but not as many as we often think.

So, ready? Go ahead, try it out and may it contribute to much love, understanding and compatibility for you and for those you care about.

COMPATIBILITY ANALYSIS WORKSHEET

Trait	First Person	Second Person	Difference
Extreme Withdrawal	_____	_____	_____
Withdrawal	_____	_____	_____
Mildly Responsive	_____	_____	_____
Responsive	_____	_____	_____
Highly Responsive	_____	_____	_____
Depth	_____	_____	_____
Cumulative Thinking	_____	_____	_____
Comprehensive Thin'g.	_____	_____	_____
Investigative Thinking	_____	_____	_____
Exploratory Thinking	_____	_____	_____
Analytical Ability	_____	_____	_____
Fluidity of Thought	_____	_____	_____
Thinking Efficiency	_____	_____	_____
Acquisitiveness	_____	_____	_____
Aggressiveness	_____	_____	_____
Argumentativeness	_____	_____	_____
Attention, Desire for	_____	_____	_____
Broad-Mindedness	_____	_____	_____
Caution	_____	_____	_____
Change, Desire for	_____	_____	_____
Clannishness	_____	_____	_____
Concentration	_____	_____	_____
Confusion of Interest	_____	_____	_____
Deceit	_____	_____	_____
Decisiveness	_____	_____	_____
Defiance	_____	_____	_____
Detail, Attention to	_____	_____	_____

Trait	First Person	Second Person	Difference
Determination	_____	_____	_____
Dignity	_____	_____	_____
Diplomacy	_____	_____	_____
Directness	_____	_____	_____
Dominating	_____	_____	_____
Domineering	_____	_____	_____
Enthusiasm	_____	_____	_____
Evasiveness	_____	_____	_____
Fatalism	_____	_____	_____
Frankness	_____	_____	_____
Generousity	_____	_____	_____
Goal Setting	_____	_____	_____
Humour	_____	_____	_____
Humour, Dry	_____	_____	_____
Idiosyncrasy	_____	_____	_____
Imagination	_____	_____	_____
Imagination, Latent	_____	_____	_____
Indecisiveness	_____	_____	_____
Independent Thinking	_____	_____	_____
Initiative	_____	_____	_____
Intuitiveness	_____	_____	_____
Irritability	_____	_____	_____
Jealousy	_____	_____	_____
Line Value	_____	_____	_____
Literary Leanings	_____	_____	_____
Manual Dexterity	_____	_____	_____
Narrow-Mindedness	_____	_____	_____
Optimism	_____	_____	_____
Organization Ability	_____	_____	_____

Trait	First Person	Second Person	Difference
Ostentation	_____	_____	_____
Persistence	_____	_____	_____
Pessimism	_____	_____	_____
Physical-Mindedness	_____	_____	_____
Positiveness	_____	_____	_____
Precision, Physical	_____	_____	_____
Pride	_____	_____	_____
Procrastination	_____	_____	_____
Regression	_____	_____	_____
Rejection	_____	_____	_____
Repression	_____	_____	_____
Resentment	_____	_____	_____
Responsibility	_____	_____	_____
Reticence	_____	_____	_____
Sarcasm	_____	_____	_____
Secretiveness	_____	_____	_____
Selectivity	_____	_____	_____
Self-Castigation	_____	_____	_____
Self-Consciousness	_____	_____	_____
Self-Deceit	_____	_____	_____
Self-Esteem	_____	_____	_____
Self-Reliance	_____	_____	_____
Sensitivity to Criticism	_____	_____	_____
Stubbornness	_____	_____	_____
Talkativeness	_____	_____	_____
Temper	_____	_____	_____
Tenacity	_____	_____	_____
Vanity	_____	_____	_____
Variety, Desire for	_____	_____	_____

Trait	First Person	Second Person	Difference
Willpower	_____	_____	_____
Worry	_____	_____	_____
Yieldingness	_____	_____	_____

9

KIDS, TEACHERS
AND PARENTS

—

This chapter deals with the kids you love and the kids in whom you might have invested a little of your ego. I hope you will recall that "no trait stands alone" and you won't jump to any hasty conclusions. The considerations I'm presenting here are generally true. However, any of them could be modified considerably by whatever else may be in a child's personality and writing. If you take these ideas as guidelines, and use your good judgment and a little objectivity, you should find some interesting information and some helpful suggestions.

Before getting into the chapter, I also want to point out that David Grayson might be one of the most knowledgeable people in North America on this subject. Dave is a school superintendent in the Chicago area and a Graphoanalyst, and, while I wrote a chapter on this subject, he wrote a book. If you ever want a speaker or a conference leader who will also entertain you, get Dave if you can. If you can't, call me. Dave can be reached at 708-848-0946, docgrayson@aol.com or at www.davegrayson.com. His book is in the bibliography.

To begin, here are two tricky situations or dilemmas that generate a good bit of debate.

First, most teachers don't realize it, but if you believe, as I do, that there is something to Graphotherapy (see page 198), then when teachers teach children one of the usual copybook methods, they are also teaching and reinforcing certain personality traits. Some of these traits may not be desirable.

Four copybook scripts that are commonly taught in Canadian and U.S. elementary schools: are The D'Nealian Method, The Palmer Method, The Zaner-Bloser Method and one from The School Zone Publishing Company.

Below I have redrawn ten examples, that I found in these copy book scripts that relate to personality traits you may wish to reconsider. They are labeled with a letter which corresponds to the short descriptions that follow.

f

A. Poor Organization Ability

h k m

B. Resentment

m n

C. Non-Analytical

o g g d

D. Directness

o

E. Secretiveness

m u w

F. Jealousy

p

G. Argumentativeness

depth

H. Independent Thinking

a a C c O o

I. Low Self-Esteem

baby

J. Little Imagination

A. All four methods have unbalanced lower case f's correlating with poor organizational ability.

B. All four methods have some rigid lead-in strokes indicating resentment.

C. The retraced downstrokes on the m's and n's in three of the methods indicate non-analytical thinking.

D. The lack of lead-in strokes on some of the lower case letters, in three of the methods, indicate directness.

E. In all cases, we can see secretiveness in the exit loop of the capital O.

F. In two of the methods, there are tight little beginning loops on some of the capital U's, V's, W's and other letters that indicate jealousy.

G. We can see an argumentative spike on the p in three of the samples.

H. In three cases, the d's and t's are short of healthy self-pride.

I. In three cases, self-esteem is low.

J. Generally the upper and the lower loops are short and narrow, displaying little imagination.

So, what is a teacher to do? Well, there aren't many options. We have to teach our children some common methods of written communication and most of us do seem to survive this dilemma. My advice is that, whichever method you use, go ahead and teach it but, as you see students begin to express their individuality, be flexible and allow it as long as it is still legible and conveys the intended meaning.

For example, if little Egbert doesn't want to retrace the downstrokes of his m's and n's, leave him to it as long as he makes clear m's and n's. Otherwise, if you insist on retracing, you might be stifling his analytical ability. As well, you will probably lose the battle over the long haul anyway because, if little Egbert really is analytical, it will show up in his m's and n's sooner or later.

If you would like to be more proactive, you could make some changes to the typical copy book script. Here are some suggestions:

A. Balance the f's. The issue, here, isn't the fullness of the loops but the distance above and below the baseline (page 79).

B. Soften the lead-ins with a gentle curve (page 91).

C. Let the kids decide if they want to retrace the downstrokes on their m's and n's (page 32).

D. Teach the lead-in strokes; if some students drop them, fine (page 54).

E. Don't worry whether secretive loops are in or out. You'll soon see them show up in those who can keep a secret and those who are not totally forthcoming (page 95).

F. Replace the jealousy stroke (page 73) and substitute a humour stroke (page 63), and make the world a happier place.

G. Get rid of the argumentative spike (page 39) and develop better listeners who will interrupt less.

H. The healthiest t's and d's generally have stems that are two to two and a half times as high as the lower case letters in height (page 86).

I. Teach capital letters that are at least two and a half times taller than the lower case letters (page 100).

J. Teach loops that are both tall and wide. Those students who won't have much imagination or ability to handle change and variety may never fall into line easily. But, who knows? Perhaps some will become more imaginative and flexible than they would have been otherwise (pages 43, 66, 108).

The other potential dilemma facing teachers is that generally, brighter people are quicker thinkers and thus, quicker writers. Often, the hand is not able to keep up with the mind and, when the hand speeds up to capture the thoughts, the writing gets sloppy. Yes, generally, the brighter people have poorer penmanship. If I cite medical doctors, may I rest my case?

Again, what is a teacher to do? Well, if the sloppy writer is bright, chances are that you want him or her to stay bright, so don't put too restrictive a harness on his/her hand. Work patiently for clear writing but be willing to trade off some sloppiness for some "smarts."

I realize that parents are also concerned about this and many feel that their child's penmanship is not as good as they think it should be. This has some validity because cursive writing is not taught in schools as much as it used to be and because keyboarding has replaced it to a considerable degree.

Incidentally, for anyone wanting to improve a child's penmanship, I highly recommend **Callirobics**. See the glossary for details.

Interesting too, among quite a few knowledgeable people, there is the idea that, in our digitized world, we are losing some important brain function when we reduce the amount of cursive writing that we do. Educational Kinesiologists and some behavioural scientists tell us that cursive writing, martial arts, meditation and certain other activities can increase the number of nerves in the corpus callosum, that mass of nerves that joins the two hemispheres of the brain. This means that handwriting and some of these other activities can enhance the integration of the two halves of the brain and thus improve overall brain performance.

So, parents and teachers, encourage lots of handwriting with your children, work to make it legible and relax if it isn't quite as you think it should be. Little Egbert and his classmates have their own personalities, their own life purposes and they are going to express them in many unique ways. Don't give them a hard time, support them, love them and enjoy them.

What follows now are some elements of handwriting analysis that I believe can help parents and teachers contribute to the learning and development of children.

The Emotions:

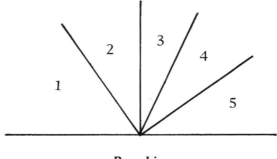

Base Line

Remember this? This is the slant gauge from page 23 and it can help us gather insights into our children's emotional responsiveness. With this information, we can then be more sensitive and more effective in providing what our children need on an emotional level.

Below, I have recorded some descriptions for each of the five areas of the gauge. After you decide the area(s) into which your child's writing fits (page 23 will show you how), consider the descriptions and respond as your good judgment suggests.

Area 1—Extreme Withdrawal: These children are hardly at all responsive emotionally. They are often quite withdrawn and find communication difficult. They do not easily reveal themselves to others until a good deal of trust is established. When you do see an expression of emotion, it may not be the true self. As well, these kids can be very egocentric with a strong "me first" attitude. When the backhandedness is this severe, it may reveal some trauma or abuse in the background.

These children have more insecurities than other children and, therefore, need more recognition and reassurance than most others—even if they don't show that they do. Encouraging them to belong to groups and participate in group activities where they have some ability and can achieve success can be helpful. These kids, more than most, need to be reminded and shown frequently that they are understood and loved.

Area 2—Withdrawal: Emotionality is still not a big part of these children's lives. The "what's in it for me" attitude is not as strong as it is with the Area 1 kids but it will surface from time to time. There is still a good deal of insecurity operating here and these kids are often somewhat withdrawn and introverted. If they appear extroverted, it's often a role they are playing, and they may not be doing it consciously.

Again, the best way to help these children is to frequently communicate and demonstrate understanding, love and encouragement. Provide situations where they can win, achieve and feel good about themselves, e.g. if they are good in sports, chess or whatever, provide opportunities and encouragement in these areas.

Area 3—Mildly Responsive: These up and down writers are ruled mostly by the head. Logic, facts, data, analysis, etc. is their way of approaching the world. They are objective, careful and generally, as far as kids go, quite controlled. They can work well under pressure and tend to be relatively calm in a crisis. The calmness these children display can often be misinterpreted as disinterest or not caring, when actually, they are assessing, analyzing and figuring out the best course of action. They won't be the cheerleaders but they will provide and easily share solutions.

Don't expect these children to jump around, expressing great enthusiasm for most of life's events. They are not disinterested, they are just more into their heads than their hearts. Don't make them the cheerleaders, assign them the roles of planner, organizer or score-keeper. These kids need to be reassured that what they do and how they do it is valid and useful.

So, find activities that suit their "head-driven" approach to life. As well, encourage them to express their feelings. They have them, they are just not inclined to express them as much as others.

Area 4—Responsive: These children have a healthy balance between the head and the heart. They are generally outgoing and approach life with both empathy and level-headedness. They usually get along well with others and are most often kind and considerate. These kids are usually steady, practical and predictable but, in a crisis, they can have difficulty staying calm.

Children whose writing exhibits this type of slant are natural helpers and you can assist them by encouraging them to engage in good deeds and support others. They need love and affection, just like anyone else, so don't hold back just because they may seem better adjusted than most.

Area 5—Highly Responsive: Emotions run high with these characters. They are usually extroverted, impulsive and full of energy. They have a tendency to jump to conclusions and make errors of haste. They are the ones who get into trouble by speaking before thinking and they are the first to lose control of their emotions.

On the positive side, they are usually charming, persuasive, warm, read people well and have many friends. They carry strong feelings about the things and people they like, and they usually make great sales people, politicians or leaders.

These children generally need more self-control and strategies for dealing with stressful or emotional events. In class, perhaps seat them with a few vertical writers, teach them about planning, organizing, weighing pros and cons, prioritizing, etc. Because they are naturally inclined towards others, it is also helpful to get them into situations where this inclination can be used, e.g. let them be the cheer leaders, the sales reps., the team leaders, the care givers, etc. It is in these areas where they will shine and their self-esteem will grow.

Sometimes, we will see a child's slant vary considerably more than the norm. This is usually a signal that something in the child's life is not going right. Varying slant means varying emotional responsiveness, often expressed as mood swings. Sometimes there is extreme responsiveness, sometimes cool detachment and, other times, pull back or withdrawal. This is not uncommon when puberty is kicking in. If the variations are due to something reasonably temporary, it should pass. If you can't put your finger on the source, professional help might be in order.

Depth, you'll recall from page 25, is the pressure that a writer puts on the paper and it indicates energy level, sensuousness and the duration of emotional memory.

The heavy writers, the ones who make impressions on the paper that you can easily feel from the other side, are the high energy types. They are usually quick off the mark, action oriented, like variety and have staying power. If you are recruiting endurance athletes, consider these characters.

These children also have heightened senses. They feel textures, hear sounds, see colour, smell scents, etc. better (barring handicaps) than the average citizen.

Probably most significant, the heavy writers have a longer term emotional memory. They will remember events that were happy, sad, angry, etc. longer than most people. It is not easy for them to "let by-gones be by-gones." They may understand intellectually that "letting go" is important and healthier but emotionally it is difficult for them.

Mood changes don't happen quickly for the heavy writers. If they are in a funk, they'll likely stay there longer. They will keep things bottled up longer and, as the pressure builds, they can be volatile and blow. Strategies such as time out or cooling off can often be helpful as well as offering opportunities to blow off steam in constructive ways, e.g. sports, exercise, etc.

By now, you are in a position to look at some emotional combinations. For example, how about a far rightward slant in combination with heavy writing? Well, it depends on what else is in the writing. If there is a lot of artistic ability, humour, sensitivity, intuitiveness, imagination, etc., you might have a pretty dynamic and interesting individual. If, on the other hand, you had anger, resentment, deceit, impatience, jealousy, sarcasm etc., you would have a very different character, wouldn't you? Again, no single trait stands alone.

Thinking Styles:

You might recall from Chapter 4 the four different thinking styles. They are illustrated below in figures A, B, C and D, and they are followed by some observations about how a teacher or parent might take them into account.

A. Cumulative

B. Comprehensive

C. Investigative

D. Exploratory

You might recall that the **cumulative** thinker is the one who is steady and a little slower to get off the mark. As the tortoise of the thinking world, he/she often finishes more creatively and more correctly than some of the quicker thinkers. Thomas Edison, who invented something like 4,999 ways a light bulb didn't work, was one of these. These thinkers take a little more time to digest a problem and begin to develop solutions.

As a teacher, when you ask a question to the class, don't call on these students first. They need a little more time to formulate their answer. Once they are ready, they will likely have one that is well thought out. As well, because these children are a little slower, self-confidence could be an issue. It's not a bad idea to remind them, from time to time, that taking their time to be careful is good and that they have many positive points to be proud of; speed just isn't one of them.

If the cumulative thinkers are the tortoises of the thinking world, the **comprehensive** thinkers are the hares. While the former are pondering the teacher's question, the latter will likely have their hands in the air before she/he has finished asking it. The comprehensive thinkers are bright, quick to catch on but sometimes prone to be hasty and jump to conclusions. That's why, as the story goes, the hare lost to the tortoise.

If you, as a teacher or parent, have one of these comprehensive thinkers, you are blessed with a bright child. They like intellectual challenges and will likely shine on the chess team, debating society and be the first out the door after writing exams. To help them, keep them challenged and/or slow them down a little by getting them into the habit of checking their work.

Both the **investigators** and the **explorers** like to learn. They probe into subjects, find out how things work and ask "why" a lot. Some like to dig deeply and understand all about a subject while others are content with more superficial knowledge on a broad number of subjects. Generally, the taller the m's and n's, the deeper the interest.

Before embracing new ideas, these thinkers generally like to check things out for themselves. They are more prone to be stuck in the mud because you told them they might get stuck if they walked in the mud. They have a lot of curiosity and this should be encouraged.

Analytical thinkers like to process information, sift through data and prioritize. In prioritizing, they easily separate the important from the unimportant, as they see it. This can be puzzling, if not frustrating to parents and teachers because they will attend to the things that they think are important and ignore the others.

men   *men*

Analytical   Non-Analytical

The good news is that, when life gets more complicated, they will be better equipped to handle what is most important first, and live with letting the unimportant slide. Analytical thinkers are usually the best managers and parents and teachers might place them into situations where they can build on this ability, e.g. putting them in charge of projects or in positions of leadership.

You can see how a grasp of thinking styles could be helpful in a variety of situations. Here's a counselling scenario: Suppose little Mildred's parents want to meet with her teacher about their child's poor performance in grade four. The parents are frustrated because when they have tried to explain Mildred's lessons to her, she just doesn't seem to catch on as quickly as they think she should. The parents are both comprehensive thinkers, the teacher is an investigator and little Mildred is a cumulative thinker. What might the teacher do to help the parents understand that it isn't in little Mildred's nature to catch on as quickly as Mom and Dad?

When forming groups to do projects or solve problems, I know teachers have a number of considerations to balance, e.g. gender, ability, behaviour, etc. It is helpful as well, to consider thinking styles. You probably don't want all of the cumulative thinkers in one group with all of the comprehensive thinkers in another group, unless you are testing some graphoanalytic hypothesis. Generally, I suspect you would be better off with a mix of thinking styles. Remember, even in a single individual, the more thinking styles you have, the greater the problem-solving potential.

Size: Remember concentration, page 45? When the writing is ¹⁄₁₆th of an inch or smaller, it indicates concentration. Children with writing this small can really focus their attention and are not easily distracted. When they are busily engaged in some project or have their noses in a book, they may never hear the call when they are summoned for lunch. These kids can really focus their attention, block out their surroundings and withdraw from others. They usually work well alone and are often quite good at tasks involving detail.

Sometimes their ability to focus can be annoying and lead the rest of us to conclude that they are being disobedient when they don't come for lunch after the first call. Chances are, they are not ignoring us, they just simply didn't hear the call. To help these kids, we need to exercise extra patience or else take extra steps to ensure that they really do hear us when we call.

Generally speaking, tiny writing points to the introverts while large writing travels with the extroverts. As the writing gets larger, we encounter the outgoing ones who enjoy others, don't sit still for long and love being the centre of attention. These individuals are often the stereotypical sales representatives.

Learning Disabilities:

It seems that today, either there really are more learning disabilities among our children or we are just more aware of them because we have more sophisticated methods for detecting them. I think there is something to both. Clearly, we do have better methods for identifying them but it also seems that, as we have more allergies, asthma and degenerative disease than ever, we also have more learning disabilities than ever.

Why? I'm not sure but it wouldn't surprise me if it had something to do with today's poorer nutritional practices. Whether it is due to all the junk food kids consume, soil depletion, the bombardment of free radicals, pollution, the lack of enzymes in vegetables, the side effects of antibiotics, etc., research tells us that these things are causing many disorders; why not learning disabilities?

Here is something that, to my knowledge, doesn't have much formal research behind it but because some credible people think it holds up quite well, I thought it worth presenting. There are four letters of the alphabet (m, n, h and k) that each strike the base line at least three times when they are written correctly, like this.

In some learning disabled individuals, there is a notable absence of a middle stroke touching the baseline. What you often see is something like this:

In my handwriting analysis class one evening, a Core Resource Teacher volunteered that, just that day, she was working with a boy who had some learning disabilities. She was helping him to improve his penmanship and it seemed that no matter how hard he tried, he just couldn't get his m's and n's to touch the baseline on all points.

My idea here is not to tell you that these four letters will replace good testing. On the contrary, effective testing by a professional is important and necessary to identify which disabilities are present, if any. At best, if you see any of these four letters consistently failing to touch the base line as they should, then some testing is likely in order to verify that disabilities exists and which ones they are.

Before this chapter becomes a book, I should start wrapping it up and point out that, although there is a great deal more that could be covered, you are capable of doing much of it yourself. Here's how: Go back to Chapter 5 and look at any one of the traits and think about how finding it in the writing and understanding it might help a child. I'm providing three examples below, Desire for Attention, Determination and Fatalism, to show you how to do it for any of the other traits.

1. ATTENTION, DESIRE FOR, PAGE 40

The stroke is the word ending that rises higher than the height of the lower-case letters and curves upward and backward.

watch me

These rising strokes could be likened to the waving of a hand, trying to attract attention. Well, thinking about it, what would help a child who is seeking attention? Why would a child seek attention?

First, observe carefully and consider whether the child really is an attention seeker and, if so, is it a serious problem? Is he/she getting into trouble? Are they constantly speaking out? Are they the class clown? If your conclusion is that the handwriting stroke has pointed to a disruptive attention seeker, then what is an appropriate reaction?

At this point, it might be appropriate for the teacher and parent/guardian to confer and commit to some remedial approach. Perhaps they will conclude that more recognition, reassurance and expressions of love are appropriate. Perhaps, there are some self-esteem issues. Maybe more opportunities to be involved in groups or activities where some victories can be achieved would be a good move. Possibly, getting professional help would be appropriate.

2. DETERMINATION, PAGE 51

The trait is identified when downstrokes, below the base line are thicker than the rest of the writing. The thickness indicates the degree of force of determination while the length indicates the endurance or staying power of the determination.

This, of course, has implications for job completion and achievement. When a child has a thick and long downstroke, we see someone who stays the course and completes the job. A thin downstroke, likely won't stay the course. A short thick downstroke indicates someone who will start strongly and may finish short term projects but who can't be counted on to finish longer term projects. The downstroke that starts strongly and weakens as it progresses, travels with the child whose endurance fades as the project continues.

An interesting one that occurs quite often in elementary school is the y or g downstroke that bends to the left. The speculation here is that the child doesn't put forth the necessary effort to complete tasks because they have learned that someone will come to the rescue and do it for them. Dave Grayson says this often occurs in grades four, five and six where parents are doing too much of the homework and are teaching their children to avoid responsibility.

If you find a lack of determination in a child's handwriting, again, probably teacher and parent should put their heads together and develop an appropriate strategy, e.g. projects of shorter duration, encouragement to stay the course, more accountability and/or recognition for finishing projects.

3. FATALISM, PAGE 59

never goes well

If you see a fair bit of this in a child's handwriting and it seems to you that something is indeed wrong, get a professional involved. Chances are that the child has a pretty negative outlook on life and needs some serious help to turn it around. You could probably say the same thing for

4. REPRESSION, PAGE 90

cannot remember how

So now, you have the idea. You look at the traits. If they appear to exist in the writing, verify them in behaviour and, if they appear to be a concern, collaborate with appropriate parties and design suitable strategies.

A final note to this chapter: Whether you are a novice or a trained and experienced handwriting analyst, you run some risk of making faulty interpretations. For this reason, please consider that your interpretations of the foregoing information could be a little off the mark. Be flexible and understand that there is much more to your child's personality than what anyone can interpret from his/her handwriting.

With this in mind, I suggest that you treat your interpretations as additional input to be considered carefully. In some cases, you might want to consult an expert, e.g. a child psychologist, guidance counselor, etc. And then, act carefully and lovingly, in the best interests of the child.

10

Signs of Potential Danger and Dishonesty

___

If this book is about self-discovery, then this chapter will definitely give you something to think about. It is a chapter that probes into our darker side and provides insight into areas that resonate with all of us. Again, as with the other chapters, this one is only an introduction to a subject that is worthy of volumes. It is another interesting area into which Handwriting Analysis can take us and it's one that intrigues everyone—danger and dishonesty.

Before proceeding, I want to make a few important points. First, you will notice that this chapter is entitled: "Signs of **Potential** Danger and Dishonesty." That's because, as far as I have been able to determine, the correlation between any one handwriting sign and danger or dishonesty has rarely, if ever, been proven beyond all doubt. As well, even if such correlations were 100% validated, they would only indicate a propensity to be dangerous or dishonest. That is to say, just because the signs may point reliably to a liar, they don't mean that the writer will lie at every opportunity, or to you. It only means that he/she has that inclination or potential.

Second, we have to be careful with correlations. One rather popular Graphologist has implied that a stroke known as the felon's claw is a sure sign of dishonesty because it appears in the writing of over 80% of convicted felons. Well, I'll bet that right-handedness also appears in over 80% of convicted felons but it doesn't mean that right-handedness is a predictor of felony. We do have to be careful with correlations and the implications we draw from them.

Third, you have read elsewhere in this book that no stroke stands alone. Well, that applies to these signs in spades. Having a high body temperature correlates with SARS. It doesn't mean, however, that everyone with a high temperature has SARS. It might, but it might also point to the flu, or infection, or something else. You need to look at the other symptoms to be sure. Similarly, I don't believe there is any single stroke or style of writing that indicates danger or dishonesty with ironclad certainty. There may be, but I believe we need to find reinforcement in the rest of the writing before pronouncing someone dangerous or dishonest.

This leads to my fourth point: Most authors on the subject state that there must be a number of indicators or signs of potential danger or dishonesty before such a pronouncement can be made. They sometimes cite a specific number such as four or seven. I have always felt that this is far too arbitrary. Surely, some indicators are more predictive of danger or dishonesty than others. To put this to a test, I met with eleven members of the Ontario Chapter of the International Graphoanalysis Society and, over the course of two days, we wrestled with approximately 60 signs in handwriting and arrived at the same conclusion, namely, some signs are more powerful indicators than others. More about this later.

Fifth, and related to the idea that no stroke stands alone, is the point that a more controlled personality will be less likely to behave dangerously or dishonestly than one who is less controlled. For example, if A and B have the exact same signs of potential danger or dishonesty in their writing, with the same frequency and intensity, but B has a number of controls such as caution, decisiveness, dignity, etc., then B is less likely to be dangerous or dishonest.

Sixth, as you know, the Creator never made duplicates. Everyone is unique and some people who engage in dangerous or dishonest acts will feel nothing at all while others would be beside themselves with great spasms of guilt feeling. This means that some dangerous or dishonest people will display nothing in their handwriting that would signal their dark side because they don't feel that it is at all dark.

Seventh, for a sign of potential danger or dishonesty to be a fair indicator, it must occur **frequently** and **consistently** in the writing.

Finally, I want to tell you how I arrived at these signs of danger and dishonesty, and my treatment of them. To begin, I searched some of the authors that you can find in the bibliography and listed most of their conclusions on the subject. Next, I convened two, one-day gatherings of the group of eleven that I mentioned earlier. This group included one of North America's best Forensic Document Examiners.

On the first day, we went over approximately 45 different signs of potential danger and dishonesty. Each analyst, based on his/her knowledge, rated each sign on a scale ranging from 0 to 10. Ten meaning: "Always indicates danger or dishonesty" and Zero meaning: "Never indicates danger or dishonesty. I totaled and averaged the scores for each sign and arranged them on a spreadsheet, ranging down the sheet, from the highest average score to the lowest. We never got any tens, the scores ranged from nine down to zero.

Upon examining this array of signs, none of us were perfectly happy with it and all felt that some fine-tuning was in order. To that end we met for the second day. We did three things that filled our day. First, we repositioned a few of the original 45 signs. Second, we slotted another 15 signs into our ranked list. And lastly, we looked at some handwriting samples that Graham Ospreay, our Forensic Document Examiner, brought from his case files (previously heard before the courts). We saw many of our 60 signs in Graham's samples.

As a group, we did one further thing. Having noticed that many authors on this subject treat most of these signs with equal weight, we decided that we could go a step further. We could clearly see that the signs rated nine were stronger indicators of potential danger or dishonesty that those rated one or two. We couldn't, however, say as easily that a five was really much stronger than a four. What we agreed to do then was draw two lines across our listing, dividing it into three sections, one that separated the threes from the fours and one that separated the sixes from the sevens. We then ended up with three sections, one that grouped the sevens, eights and nines together; another that grouped the fours, fives and sixes; and a final section that was made up of the ones, twos and threes. We decided to label the first section "Strong Signs of Potential Danger and Dishonesty." We called the second section "Moderate Signs of Potential Danger and Dishonesty." And, the third section was termed "Mild Signs of Potential Danger and Dishonesty."

Our group would like more time to expand, fine-tune and further test our scheme. I hope we do find that time, as I am sure it will significantly improve our model. In the meantime, however, I had a publishing deadline to meet and, so, I ran with the group's current product, added five more signs, did a small amount of fine-tuning and presented the signs as you see them below.

A final point: Although there were some very credible and experienced people involved with this study, and we drew upon the conclusions of well-recognized authors, our study was not scientific, nor are very many of the conclusions presented by the other authors. The conclusions, however, are pretty generally accepted in the Graphology community and are about as credible as we are likely to get. Clearly, more research is required and there are a great many directions in which it can go. One example might be to engineer this model a little further and, after sufficient testing, assign points to the categories. Let's say, for example, we determine that the strong signs are worth ten points each, the moderate signs are worth five points each and the mild signs get two each. Again, with further study, we might then be able to say something like: "A writer must score at least 30 points before he/she can be declared "Potentially Dangerous or Dishonest." Well... something to think about and, as so many studies wind up saying: "Further research required."

In presenting each of the signs below, I have offered a description of the sign, an hypothesis about its meaning and an illustration to show what it looks like. I use the term hypothesis because, as I said before, this is not based on science but rather on the interpretations that are widely accepted by members of the Graphology community. Here they are:

Strong Signs of Potential Danger or Dishonesty:

None of these signs by themselves constitute enough evidence to point the finger and declare someone either dangerous or dishonest. Although these are among the strongest signs Graphology can identify, by themselves, they are not strong enough. They are strong enough, however, that when they appear frequently and consistently in the writing, they should raise some serious doubt and prompt the analyst to look further for reinforcing signs. The probabilities are high, that when you see one of these signs frequently and consistently in a sample of writing, it won't be difficult to find others.

1. DESCRIPTION: Openings in circle letters on or near the baseline.

    HYPOTHESIS: The writer lacks integrity and is not to be trusted.

    ILLUSTRATION:

    good boy John

2. DESCRIPTION: Approach strokes and final strokes both form loops within circle letters.

    HYPOTHESIS: This writer is deceitful and conceals or misrepresents the truth either intentionally or unintentionally, through either words or actions. He may misrepresent facts to avoid disapproval from others. He frequently tells people what he believes they want to hear.

ILLUSTRATION:

3. DESCRIPTION: A loop on the interior, left side of lower case circle letters combined with an interior single or double hook.

HYPOTHESIS: This writer is manipulative, intentionally deceptive and scheming in order to get her own way. She could also be a compulsive liar.

ILLUSTRATION:

4. DESCRIPTION: Figure eights in the top of lower case circle letters.

HYPOTHESIS: This writer purposefully misrepresents the truth and could also be a compulsive liar.

ILLUSTRATION:

5. DESCRIPTION: An unusual space between two words.

HYPOTHESIS: This writer is hesitating in order to "get the story straight." The word or words following the space are often misleading.

ILLUSTRATION: *I only took   three*

6. DESCRIPTION: Low form writing with pronounced threads.
   HYPOTHESIS: Such a writer is erratic and unreliable.
   ILLUSTRATION: *I have no memory of children*

7. DESCRIPTION: Pressure that varies from light to heavy.
   HYPOTHESIS: This writer's energy is up and down and her behaviour is unpredictable and erratic. She can be calm one moment and raging the next. She could be on drugs. If the heavy pressure shows up on only a few words, those words might have significant meaning for the writer.
   ILLUSTRATION: *I cannot remember if I went*

8. DESCRIPTION: Very heavy pressure applied to punctuation, known as dot grinding.
   HYPOTHESIS: This obsessive writer often harbours deep resentment and can be either the perpetrator
   ILLUSTRATION: *make my day !*
   Police, Don't SHOOT !

9. DESCRIPTION: Long initial strokes that begin below the baseline with a hook or barb, known as harpoons.

   HYPOTHESIS: This writer has deep resentment that can manifest in violent behaviour.

   ILLUSTRATION:

   good boy

10. DESCRIPTION: Curved wedge formations known as shark's teeth.

    HYPOTHESIS: This writer appears to be pleasant and friendly but will not give you a straight answer. He is a back-stabber and is always out to achieve his own agenda. Writer is not to be trusted with the truth.

    ILLUSTRATION:

    who is missing ?

11. DESCRIPTION: Lower case d-stems that slant far more to the right than the rest of the writing. This stroke is sometimes referred to as the maniac d.

    HYPOTHESIS: This writer can lose control and give in to fits of rage.

    ILLUSTRATION:

    wasn't good enough

12. DESCRIPTION: Overly complex or exaggerated strokes, exclusive of signatures.

    HYPOTHESIS: This writer is obscuring or misrepresenting the truth.

    ILLUSTRATION: *Toppled it*

13. DESCRIPTION: Strokes that coil counterclockwise into the centre.

    HYPOTHESIS: This writer is vane, egocentric or both and will exaggerate and/or lie to make himself look good.

    ILLUSTRATION: *forgive*

14. DESCRIPTION: Downstrokes below the baseline that get progressively thicker as they approach their end, known as the club stroke.

    HYPOTHESIS: The thickening signals a sudden rise in the emotions. Such writers are explosive and dangerous.

    ILLUSTRATION: *going forgetting*

15. DESCRIPTION: Cross or X strokes that appear in unexpected places.

    HYPOTHESIS: This writer enjoys conflict and confrontation. Particularly significant when in a signature, the personal pronoun I or when below the baseline.

    ILLUSTRATION: *me too boy*

Moderate Signs of Potential Danger or Dishonesty:

Many of these signs can point to personality traits that can be either negative or positive. For exmple, #8, a defiant person may express her defiance by standing up to an injustice rather than flaunting the rules, or #10, a secretive person may be the ideal candidate for a job that requires confidences to be kept. When these signs appear frequently and consistently in a sample of writing, it is only fair to question the integrity of the writer. If none of the strong signs appear in the sample, then I suspect you need at least a half dozen or more other signs before you can be sure you have a potentially dangerous or dishonest character.

1. DESCRIPTION: Single letters that drop below the baseline, especially the personal pronoun I.

    HYPOTHESIS: At an unconscious level, this writer has negative drives and appetites that will manifest in either her philosophy of life, code of ethics or behaviour.

    ILLUSTRATION: *Bob didn't say*

2. DESCRIPTION: Interior hooks at the top of circle letters. They may be either a double hook or a single initial hook.

   HYPOTHESIS: This writer is evasive and gets around the truth without actually telling a lie.

   ILLUSTRATION:

   g o a d

3. DESCRIPTION: Exceptionally heavy downstrokes below the baseline, much heavier than determination.

   HYPOTHESIS: This writer is a bluffer. He brags about his ability to do more than he can do or intends to do.

   ILLUSTRATION:

   going forgetting

4. DESCRIPTION: Hooked Es, sometimes referred to as Spoon Es. The initial stroke is a straight upstroke, followed by a counter clockwise curve that begins with a short retracing of the upstroke.

   HYPOTHESIS: This writer pauses in mid-stroke to calculate his devious plan. The plan usually involves some distortion of the truth and some sudden move when least expected.

   ILLUSTRATION:

   e

5.   DESCRIPTION: Smeared, muddy writing with blobs, blotches, cross outs and partially filled-in circles and loops.

    HYPOTHESIS: This writer has extreme sensual appetites, e.g. food, drink, sex, combined with built up emotional pressure. She is impulsive and prone to lying.

    ILLUSTRATION:

good going Bob

6.   DESCRIPTION: Retraced hook on the last mound of an M or N.

    HYPOTHESIS: This writer is clever at taking advantage of others for his own gain.

    ILLUSTRATION:

mine not yours

7.   DESCRIPTION: Downward sloping T-bars with pointed right ends.

    HYPOTHESIS: The writer exercises control over others and, in so doing, uses methods that would be characterized as domineering, tyrannical, over-bearing, exploitive, etc.

    ILLUSTRATION:

tell a tall tale

8. DESCRIPTION: The buckle on a lower-case k is higher than other lower-case letters.

   HYPOTHESIS: This writer is defiant and may feel that the rules do not apply to her.

   ILLUSTRATION:

   keep taking

9. DESCRIPTION: Ambiguous letters and numbers.

   HYPOTHESIS: The writer is attempting to deceive.

   ILLUSTRATION: *9   5   U   2l*

10. DESCRIPTION: A loop on the interior, right side of lower case circle letters.

    HYPOTHESIS: This writer is secretive and likes to keep things to himself. Although he can keep a confidence, he is also capable of withholding important information.

    ILLUSTRATION:

    good cat

11. DESCRIPTION: The downward stroke of a circle letter starts beyond the mouth of the letter. Sometimes referred to as the cover up stroke.

    HYPOTHESIS: This writer is careful about what she says and how she says it, and will often conceal or cover up the truth.

    ILLUSTRATION: *dog ate*

12. DESCRIPTION: Twisted upper loops.

    HYPOTHESIS: This writer's thinking can be twisted or warped and he may have a twisted philosophy or approach to morality.

    ILLUSTRATION: *tall tale*

13. DESCRIPTION: Extremely heavy pressure on the page that leaves very deep impressions in the paper.

    HYPOTHESIS: This writer combines very strong energy with frustration and can erupt easily. May also have dependencies on drugs or alcohol.

    ILLUSTRATION: *too heavy*

14. DESCRIPTION: Stabs and jabs that appear in circle letters.
    HYPOTHESIS: Circle letters relate to the sending of communication. These writers are prone to lying.
    ILLUSTRATION:

    one - on - one

15. DESCRIPTION: A thread of very light pressure that appears in the middle of a word.
    HYPOTHESIS: This writer feels pushed down and overwhelmed. Her first interest is survival. She dodges responsibility and is opportunistic. If the writing is illegible, she has little feeling for the welfare of others.
    ILLUSTRATION:

    a thread of pressure

16. DESCRIPTION: A straight downstroke below the baseline that ends in a claw-like arcade to the left. This stroke is frequently referred to as the felon's claw.
    HYPOTHESIS: This writer is in some kind of confining situation, either physical or psychological. He is probably carrying a good deal of guilt feeling and may have some fixation on a more pleasant past. Could be either a victim or perpetrator.
    ILLUSTRATION:

    going far away

17. DESCRIPTION: A short initial stroke that forms a sharp angle with the next stroke. This stroke is often referred to as a temper tick. The temper is stronger when the writing is heavier.

    HYPOTHESIS: This writer is susceptible to losing her temper.

    ILLUSTRATION: *Which man talks*

18. DESCRIPTION: Slow, deliberate, drawn writing.

    HYPOTHESIS: This writer is being very cautious and deliberate, taking time to "get the story straight" or attempting to hide the real person.

    ILLUSTRATION: *don't do it*

19. DESCRIPTION: An oblong, lower case g that sits diagonally on the baseline and has a curved downstroke that goes leftward under the baseline, staying below the baseline and looking like a reversed c.

    HYPOTHESIS: Under the guise of a nice person, this cunning and devious writer purposefully sets out to achieve his own ends with no regard to the welfare of others.

    ILLUSTRATION: *going to go*

20. DESCRIPTION: Distortions, twists and sharp angles below the baseline.

HYPOTHESIS: These writers have unconventional physical or sexual desires and/or fantasies, and, if acting on them, may violate others.

ILLUSTRATION: *going your way*

Mild Signs of Potential Danger or Dishonesty:

Nearly every one of us has made some of these signs frequently and consistently in a sample of handwriting. For these to point to a potentially dangerous or dishonest person, the sample would need to also have either a large number of these mild signs, or a significant number of moderate and/or strong signs occurring frequently and consistently in the sample.

1. DESCRIPTION: Uneven or wavy baseline.
   HYPOTHESIS: This writer is unstable, moody and unreliable.
   ILLUSTRATION: *the girl flew over the fence*

2. DESCRIPTION: Formless, illegible text.
   HYPOTHESIS: Unless there is good evidence of speed, the writer wants to hide the truth, cover it up or otherwise misdirect the reader.
   ILLUSTRATION:

   what was he going to do when he got

3. DESCRIPTION: Long leftward ending strokes above the baseline.

   HYPOTHESIS: This writer has a "me first" attitude and likes to draw attention to herself. When the stroke is a T-bar, she is focused on the past and can carry a good deal of self-blame or guilt feeling where there may or may not be any real guilt.

   ILLUSTRATION: *she says she'll go*

4. DESCRIPTION: Very tight, pinched, horizontally compressed writing.

   HYPOTHESIS: This writer is tense and inhibited. He is stingy, withholds his feelings and lacks generosity. He could cheat to hold on to his money.

   ILLUSTRATION: *I intend to keep it to myself*

5. DESCRIPTION: Distinct difference between a signature and text.

   HYPOTHESIS: With the signature, this writer is attempting to present a personality to the public that is different than who she really is.

   ILLUSTRATION: *I remain yours very truly*

   Olive Smith

6. DESCRIPTION: A loop on the interior, left side of lower case circle letters.

   HYPOTHESIS: The writer is deceiving himself and does not face facts realistically. He can rationalize his actions, make compromises within himself and is often in a state of denial.

   ILLUSTRATION:

7. DESCRIPTION: Illegible signature.

   HYPOTHESIS: Writers who are in a hurry or sign their name frequently may develop a quick scrawl. Otherwise, the writer is hiding and/or does not want to be recognized.

   ILLUSTRATION:

8. DESCRIPTION: Small, tight, initial loops that start in a flat-bottomed leftward, clockwise direction, sometimes referred to as the jealousy stroke.

   HYPOTHESIS: This writer feels inadequate and doubts her ability to compete for the approval of others. Out-performing or looking better than others is important to her.

   ILLUSTRATION:

9. DESCRIPTION: Below the baseline, a strong move of the upstroke that breaks sharply away from the downstroke and drives up and to the right.

    HYPOTHESIS: This writer is aggressive and can dominate and attack others. This could be desirable in contact sports but not likely so in many other arenas of society.

    ILLUSTRATION:

10. DESCRIPTION: Leftward ending downstrokes on final arcades.

    HYPOTHESIS: This writer can be insincere and calculating and tends to cover up or hide.

    ILLUSTRATION:

11. DESCRIPTION: Hooks found at the beginning of a stroke, usually found at the beginning of a word.

    HYPOTHESIS: The writer is acquisitive and likes to acquire or possess things that may be either tangible or intangible. This can be perfectly innocent as in a collector of postage stamps but it can extend to stealing.

    ILLUSTRATION: I will take it

12. DESCRIPTION: Exaggerated, large loops.
    HYPOTHESIS: The writer is so imaginative that she may have lost touch with reality.
    ILLUSTRATION:

    baby tell him

13. DESCRIPTION: Multiple corrections, touch-ups, retracting and backtracking.
    HYPOTHESIS: This writer feels inferior and defensive and is trying to improve upon the impression he is making, often representing himself as more than he is.
    ILLUSTRATION:

    he never mistakes

14. DESCRIPTION: Straight, rigid approach strokes that start at or below the baseline.
    HYPOTHESIS: This writer carries resentment for past hurts, real or imagined. In some cases, there can be an inclination to retaliate.
    ILLUSTRATION:

    letting go is tough

15. DESCRIPTION: A far rightward slant without controls.
    HYPOTHESIS: This writer is very emotionally responsive, she is impulsive and can act before considering the consequences. When combined with heavy pressure, she can be explosive.
    ILLUSTRATION: *I feel out of control*

16. DESCRIPTION: Lower-case letters that become increasingly taller within a word and, sometimes, from one word to the next.
    HYPOTHESIS: This writer lacks tact, has an inferiority complex and will tend to inflate the truth to impress others.
    ILLUSTRATION: *mission impossible*

17. DESCRIPTION: Missing letters in a word.
    HYPOTHESIS: This could be a sign of a learning disability, speed or else the writer is distressed and not easily able to concentrate. He is often careless and may omit pertinent information.
    ILLUSTRATION: *on or two presetations*

18. DESCRIPTION: Distorted or misshapened personal pronoun I.
    HYPOTHESIS: The writer has trouble with her self-concept, possibly because of dishonest activity or because of disturbing preoccupations.
    ILLUSTRATION:

19. DESCRIPTION: Both ends of a stand-alone T-bar are bent upward.
    HYPOTHESIS: This writer has little purpose in life and tends to have a blasé attitude about most things in life. He ducks responsibility and can be unreliable.
    ILLUSTRATION: *tell tall tales*

20. DESCRIPTION: Very narrow or retraced upper loops.
    HYPOTHESIS: This writer is very inhibited and constricted in her abstract and moral thinking, and has an inclination to lie.
    ILLUSTRATION: *tell tall tales*

21. DESCRIPTION: Extreme back slant.
    HYPOTHESIS: The writer is withdrawn, rarely shows his true feelings and can have a strong "me first" attitude. He can withdraw and withhold important information.
    ILLUSTRATION: *I am doing it for me*

22. DESCRIPTION: Upper and middle area downstrokes not touching the baseline.
    HYPOTHESIS: This writer might have a learning disability. Whether she does or not, she tends to leave things unfinished and may not be reliable.
    ILLUSTRATION: *his hand makes*

23. DESCRIPTION: Inconsistent letter size in the middle area.
    HYPOTHESIS: This writer is erratic, inconsistent and unpredictable, and consequently, not reliable.
    ILLUSTRATION: *remember the mission*

24. DESCRIPTION: Excessively wide Es and circle letters.
    HYPOTHESIS: This writer is exceptionally open-minded and naïve, to the point of being easily influenced and led astray.
    ILLUSTRATION:

come over here

25. DESCRIPTION: Disproportionately large circle formations on the lower case letter d.
    HYPOTHESIS: This writer doesn't care about the opinions of others and can be defy society's norms and authority.
    ILLUSTRATION:

don't dare do it

26. DESCRIPTION: Strokes that turn in the opposite direction to the one that is normal.
    HYPOTHESIS: If a normally rightward stroke goes left, the writer may be seeking comfort from her past. If the stroke is rightward where it would normally be leftward, she could be rebelling.
    ILLUSTRATION:

you go for it

27. DESCRIPTION: Upside down circle letters.

HYPOTHESIS: These strokes could be a sign of fluidity of thought. On the other hand, they may signal worry or underhandedness.

ILLUSTRATION: *go to the moon*

28. DESCRIPTION: Repeated errors and omissions in the writing.

HYPOTHESIS: Aside from any learning disabilities, something is breaking down. The words in which the errors or omissions are made may have some significance for the writer or he may be purposly misrepresenting the truth.

ILLUSTRATION: *matthw can't go*

29. DESCRIPTION: Lower case letters in the middle of words that rise up into the upper area, sometimes referred to as pop-up letters.

HYPOTHESIS: This can signal someone with a roving eye who is checking out the gender of preference or someone who is otherwise looking around for trouble.

ILLUSTRATION: *prepare to enjoy*

30. DESCRIPTION: Capital letters in place of lower case letters.
    HYPOTHESIS: This writer has a rebellious attitude and may engage in crude, anti-social behaviour to either gain attention, flaunt the rules or both.
    ILLUSTRATION:

never deceive Him

You now have a good sampling of the signs in handwriting that can point to potential danger or dishonesty. You may not agree with the way they have been organized into the three groups, and I am sure that I could be persuaded to reposition some of them, but the main idea is that all of these signs can be "red flags" that signal the writer's potential for danger or dishonesty. The more of these sign that show up in the writer's script, the more the likelihood that danger or dishonesty exists. As well, the more the signs come from the stronger end of the model, the more the reason for suspicion.

Finally, again, please remember that all of these signs must be frequently and consistently seen in the writing, and other signs must support them before you can point the finger. If you do not observe this principle, then you are being dangerous and dishonest.

Note:

The other members of our little study group were:

Grace Bly

Paul Boivin

Ruth Glidden

Elmer Hagley

Carmen Kirschling

Mary Ann Matthews

Florence Mitchell

Graham Ospreay

Leonard Ryan

Betty Ward

Cathy Weeks

My thanks to all of you and I do hope we find the opportunity to take our initial efforts further.

A final note to the book: Please remember that this book is only an introduction to handwriting analysis and there is a great deal more to be learned. I hope your curiosity will guide you to some good books and to some of the truly great teachers of this subject, so that your insights will expand and your analysis will be rich. I hope too, that this adventure in self–discovery will give you many years of satisfaction, a few answers and many more questions.

11

GLOSSARY

—

GLOSSARY

Analytical Ability:
The capacity to sift and sort through information to determine its value and to separate the important from the unimportant. It is a component of intelligence and is similar to reasoning ability.

Approach Stroke:
The stroke that leads into a letter from the base line. In many cases, approach strokes are omitted and letters are formed by beginning with a downstroke, e.g., an "a" would be started from the top of the circle with a movement downward towards the base line.

BarOn EQ-i:
The BarOn EQ-i is the first scientifically developed and validated measure of Emotional Intelligence. It is distributed by Multi-Health Systems Inc.

Base line:
It is the imaginary horizontal line upon which a letter sits. It is constructed by joining the starting point of the approach stroke to the ending point of the last downstroke. Where there is no approach stroke, the ending point of the last downstroke of the previous letter may be taken. Where there is no preceding letter, such a point may be estimated, taking into account the general line of writing. Correctly speaking, each letter has its own base line. Sometimes, the term is used to describe an imaginary line that generally underlines a word or even a line of writing.

Buckle:
The circle portion of a p or the circle and tie section of a k.

Callirobics:

Liora Laufer developed a kit called Callirobics that employs music and a series of exercises designed to improve penmanship. I have heard both teachers and parents speak highly of it. Callirobics can be ordered in Canada from Positive Strokes at (416) 446-2903, hwriting@ interlog.com or www.interlog.com/~hwriting. In the U.S., you can get it at 1-800-769-2891, calavir @cfw.com or www.callirobics.com.

Circle Letters:

Those letters that contain a circle within their structure, e.g. a, d, g, o and q.

Compatibility:

The ability to live together in relative harmony and without undue conflict.

Comprehensive Thinking:

A thinking style where the thinker easily and quickly grasps ideas, facts and information.

Cumulative Thinking:

A style of thinking that involves the gathering of facts, data and information and building methodically to a conclusion. Thinkers with this style appear to be slower than those exhibiting other thinking styles.

Cursive Writing:

Writing in which the letters are joined. Typically taught in Canadian and U.S. schools in grade three.

Depth:

The term used to describe the heaviness or weight with which the pen is pressed onto the paper. The heavier the writing, the deeper and longer lasting are the emotions. It is also an indicator of sensuousness and energy level.

Downstroke:

A stroke that moves in a downward direction, e.g. the portion of a d that starts at the top of the loop, and falls to the base line.

Emotional Intelligence:

Multi-Health Systems Inc. defines Emotional Intelligence as an array of noncognitive capabilities, competencies, and skills that influence one's ability to succeed in coping with environmental demands and pressures.

Emotional Expressiveness:

The degree to which an individual outwardly shows or expresses his or her internal response to an emotional situation. For example, the emotionally expressive person might weep when hearing a sad story.

Emotional Responsiveness:

An individual's capacity to respond to that which arouses the emotions. An emotionally responsive person, for example, is one who would feel moved by a sad story more than the average person.

Evaluated Traits:

An evaluated trait is one that is made up from combining a number of basic traits. For example, "Ambition" is evaluated or judged from a composite of the basic traits: goal–setting, acquisitiveness, self-confidence, desire for responsibility, initiative, pride, and will power. Such traits as enthusiasm, determination, aggressiveness and persistence can be supportive.

Exploratory Thinking:

A style of thinking where the thinker probes deeply into a subject with the objective of discovering new facts and information about the subject.

Final Stroke:
The last or terminal stroke of a letter, word or series of strokes.

Graphoanalysis:
The form of Handwriting Analysis that is practiced and taught by the International Graphoanalysis Society.

Graphology:
This is the generic term for "Handwriting Analysis." Abbe Jean-Hippolyte Michon, of Paris, France, was likely the first to use the term in 1878 when he published *The Practical System of Graphology.*

Graphotherapy:
William Preyer, at the University of Berlin, after demonstrating similarities between the writing of an individual's hands, teeth, feet and crook-of-the-elbow, proclaimed that all writing is "brainwriting." His idea was that the brain sends impulses along the nervous system to the hand or to whatever is doing the writing.

This spawned the idea that the process could be reversed, suggesting that if you change the writing, you could change behavior and develop new habits.

This has not yet been validated but I believe it can work and I know individuals who claim to have used it quite successfully. One explained that she uses it, in conjunction with psychologists, in a U.S. prison system, working with inmates to build self-esteem, attention to detail, and other favourable traits.

As well, teachers and parents report that children using Callirobics demonstrate improvements in self-esteem, organizational ability, small motor coordination and attention to detail.

Graphotherapy sounds great but remember, people's personalities are the way they are for reasons that may not be apparent to the amateur. Tampering with them is the work of psychotherapy and, in this area, amateurs can be dangerous.

International Graphoanalysis Society:

The IGAS was founded by Milton Newman Bunker in 1929. It is the organization that taught and practiced Graphoanalysis. See "Grapho-analysis." They are currently going through a change in ownership and management. They can be contacted through www.igas.com.

International Graphology Association:

The IGA is a not-for-profit association for graphologists. It provides training and examination in the subject as well as undertaking research, maintaining standards of members and raising awareness of the subject. It has members in a number of countries. Further details can be obtained from the Association at Stonedge, Dunkerton, Bath BA2 8AS, England. Telephone: 01761 437809 (from abroad: 011 44 1761 437809), Facsimile: 01761 432572 (from abroad: 011 44 1761 432572). E-mail: ljw@graphology.org.uk.

Investigative Thinking:

A style of thinking where the thinker probes deeply into a subject with the objective of discovering known facts and information about the subject.

Loop:

An area of space bounded by an upstroke and a downstroke. In the upper area, loops can be found in b's, d's, f's, h's, k's, l's and t's. In the lower area, loops are generally found in f's, g's, j's, p's, q's and y's.

Lower/Material Area:

The area of writing that lies below the base line. It is here that we see how the writer acts in the physical world and how he/she seeks new experiences and friendships. It is the realm of action, instincts, urges, desires, the body, sex, health and practical imagination.

Lower–case:
The term lower–case is applied to those letters that are not capital letters.

Middle/Mundane Area:
The area of writing that is bounded by the base line and the tops of the lower case letters. It is the domain of the ego, the here and now, of daily life and of the self.

Multi-Health Systems Inc:
Dr. Steven Stein, Ph.D., is the founder and president of Multi-Health Systems Inc. MHS distributes more than 70 different assessment and diagnostic products, and has the world distribution rights for the BarOn EQ-i. MHS is located at: 3770 Victoria Park Ave, Toronto Ontario, M2H 3M6 and can be contacted at: 1-800-268-6011, customer_service@mhs.com or www.mhs.com.

Reliability:
Is a statistical measure of the degree of dependability, consistency or stability of an instrument or test upon successive trials. For example, if an individual scores 25 on a test yesterday, 50 today and 150 tomorrow, the test is not to be relied upon. But 50, 49 and 51 is much more reliable.

Upper/Abstract Area:
The area of writing that is above the tops of the lower–case letters. It is the domain of the mind or head. It is where we deal with concepts, abstractions, ideas, fantasies, philosophies, theories, spiritual elements and abstract imagination.

Upstroke:

Any stroke that rises upward.

Validity:

Is a statistical measure of the accuracy with which an instrument or test measures what it is supposed to measure. A valid test, then, is one that would be a good predictor of performance on the job. For example, let's say that someone scores a high mark on a test that is designed to predict success as a crane operator. If that person subsequently performs successfully as a crane operator, and if the test can repeatedly predict successful performance, then we can say that the test is valid.

12

BIBLIOGRAPHY

—

BIBLIOGRAPHY

Atkinson, Rita L., et al. *Introduction to Psychology.* Tenth Edition. Orlando, Florida. Harcourt Brace Jovanovich Publishers. 1990.

Crumbaugh, James C. *Graphoanalytic Cues.* Encyclopedia of Clinical Assessment, Volume II, Jossey–Bass Inc. Publishers, 1980, pp 919–929

Funk & Wagnalls. *Standard College Dictionary, Canadian Edition.* Toronto, Ontario. Longmans Canada Limited. 1963.

Goleman, Daniel. *Emotional Intelligence.* New York, N.Y. Bantam Books. October, 1995.

Grayson, David. *Better Understanding Your Child Through Handwriting.* Dak Park, Illinois. GBC Publishing. 1981.

Hilgard, Ernest R. *Introduction to Psychology.* Third Edition. New York & Burlingame. Harcourt, Brace & World, Inc. 1962.

Holmes Hatfield, Iris. *A Question of Honesty.* Louisville, KY. HuVista International Inc. 1988.

Iannetta, Kimon S., Craine, James F. and McLaughlin, Dennis. *Danger Between the Lines.* U.S.A. Private Publication.

Leslie, Edith K. *Graphology, An Outline.* Article. Toronto, Ontario. 1993.

Lowe, Sheila. *The Complete Idiot's Guide to Handwriting Analysis.* New York, New York. Alpha Books. 1999.

Mahony, Ann. *Handwriting and Personality.* New York. Ivy Books, Published by Ballantine Books. 1990.

McNichol, Andrea. *Handwriting Analysis, Putting It to Work for You.* Chicago, Illinois. Contemporary Books Inc. 1991.

Multi-Health Systems Inc. *EQ-i Certification Program.* Toronto, On. Publishers Multi-Health Systems Inc. 1997.

Nevo, Baruch. *Scientific Aspects of Graphology.* Springfield, Illinois, U.S.A. Charles C. Thomas. 1986.

Owens, Lorraine. *Handwriting Analysis: Dual Aspects of Traits.* Kansas City, Mo. 64126. Kaleidoscope Industries. 1987.

Richelyn, Roger. *To Land A Position in Paris, Penmanship Can Be Paramount.* The Wall Street Journal. September, 1985.

Sackheim, Kathryn K. *Handwriting Analysis and The Employee Selection Process.* New York. Quorum Books. 1990.

Saudek, Robert. *Experiments With Handwriting, Reprint Edition.* Sacrament, CA. Books For Professionals. 1978

The International Graphoanalysis Society. *The Encyclopedic Dictionary for Graphoanalysis.* Third Edition. Chicago, Illinois. The International Graphoanalysis Society Inc. 1988.

The International Graphoanalysis Society. *Evaluated Traits of Graphoanalysis.* Chicago, Illinois. The International Graphoanalysis Society Inc. 1992.

The International Graphoanalysis Society. *The General Course in Graphoanalysis, Lessons One Through Twenty.* Chicago, Illinois 60606. The International Graphoanalysis Society Inc. 1986.

The International Graphoanalysis Society. *Questions and Answers about Graphoanalysis.* Chicago, Illinois 60606. The International Graphoanalysis Society Inc. 1994.

The New Lexicon Webster's Encyclopedic Dictionary of The English Language, Canadian Edition. New York. Lexicon Publications Inc. 1988.

Whiting, Eldene and Lowerison, Jean. *Honesty.* Self-published, 1978.

13

INDEX

Also by *Peter* *Dennis*

METAPHYSICS
An Adventure in Self-Discovery

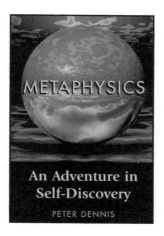

Trade Paperback • 160 pages • ISBN 0-9698926-5-9
U.S.A. $12.95 • Canada $16.95 • U.K. £8.95

Available online as well as through bookstores and all major distributors.

This book starts with the premise that we are spiritual beings existing in a physical universe, each with a specific purpose. It explains the nature of creation and our role in it, and it sheds considerable light on many of life's "Bigger Questions," e.g. Who are we? What is our purpose? Who or what created everything? What is the Creator's purpose?

As well, this book provides clear explanations for many of the concepts that are important to understanding our own spiritual nature, e.g. reincarnation, spirit guides, angels, the densification of energy, past life regression, channeling, dreams, laws of the universe, dis-ease, healing, extraterrestrials, meditation, achieving goals, creating the future and a whole host of others.

As we learn more about these concepts, we understand better where we fit in, we become more the architect of our destiny and less the victim of chance. As well, we can glimpse the beauty, order and magnificence of the divine plan. Indeed, developing these understandings is a great adventure, and in time, it becomes clear that it is mostly one of self-discovery. Enjoy the adventure.